From Isolation to Intimacy

From Isolation to Intimacy

Making Friends without Words

Phoebe Caldwell
with
Jane Horwood

Jessica Kingsley Publishers
London and Philadelphia

First published in 2007
by Jessica Kingsley Publishers
116 Pentonville Road
London N1 9JB, UK
and
400 Market Street, Suite 400
Philadelphia, PA 19106, USA

www.jkp.com

Library of Congress Cataloging in Publication Data
Caldwell, Phoebe.
    From isolation to intimacy : making friends without words / Phoebe Caldwell ; with Jane Horwood.
        p. ; cm.
    Includes bibliographical references and index.
    ISBN-13: 978-1-84310-500-8 (pbk. : alk. paper)
    ISBN-10: 1-84310-500-4 (pbk. : alk. paper) 1. Autism--Patients--Rehabilitation. 2. Learning disabled--Rehabilitation. 3. Nonverbal communication. 4. Interpersonal relations. 5. Intimacy (Psychology) I. Horwood, Jane, 1961- II. Title.
    [DNLM: 1. Autistic Disorder--therapy--Case Reports. 2. Interpersonal Relations--Case Reports. 3. Learning Disorders--therapy--Case Reports. 4. Nonverbal Communication--Case Reports. WM 203.5 C147fa 2007]
    RC553.A88C352 2007
    616.85'88206--dc22
                                2006038060

British Library Cataloguing in Publication Data
A CIP catalogue record for this book is available from the British Library

ISBN 978 1 84310 500 8

Printed and bound in the United States by Thomson-Shore, Inc.

Geraint Ephraim, psychologist at Harperbury Hospital. In the 1980s Geraint introduced the idea of using body language to communicate with non-verbal people.

Contents

Introduction

This book is about how we get in touch with people who are separated from us because they cannot tell us what they want or, perhaps more importantly, how they feel. We appear to have no point of contact with each other. Whatever their experience of the world, psychologically speaking they have to do it on their own. While we try to provide for their needs, they are without friends in the sense that we understand this, friends who will enrich our lives, share fun with us and provide support when things look bad. With them we are unlikely ever to have an adventurous relationship which mutually explores and deepens our sense of worth. Or so it seems.

Based on work with people with severe learning disability or autism (or in some cases both), *From Isolation to Intimacy* seeks to show that we can use body language, ours and theirs, to build a bridge between us, leading to a conversation that takes us right to the centre of their emotional world, the shared 'playground' where we can get to know and deeply enjoy each other's company.

All of us are different. In some ways it is more straightforward to engage with someone who simply has learning disability than with someone on the autistic spectrum, since in the latter case, in addition to any deficit they may or may not have, relationship is in itself a problem for them. So how can we get close to each other?

I am not autistic but neurotypical, neither did I set out to work particularly with people on the spectrum, but having learned to use body language with those who are non-verbal, I found myself more and more drawn into this field. Inevitably I have had to borrow from the extraordinarily penetrating writings of people who are autistic and have opened up the world of autism. Among the authors from whom I have learned particularly are Donna Williams, Temple Grandin, Gunilla Gerland, Lindsay Weekes, Wendy Lawson and Kamran Nazeer. Their thoughts have become the backcloth for reflection on the lives of people with whom I am asked to work.

My work involves both practice and teaching, so that much of the work I describe is a three-way partnership between myself, the people I have taught and the people we are trying to help. For reasons of confidentiality I cannot always identify all those whose consistent hard work has carried on such approaches as I have been able to initiate. Without their commitment, no amount of theory would effect the astonishing changes that this way of working makes possible. However, I do particularly want to thank Kelly Rayner, for her detailed account of the dedicated follow-up work she did with Niall. There is no doubt that without her interventions he would still be one of the most distressed individuals I have ever met. I also need to thank Kaj Kristiansen, Suzanne Oppelstrup and Davy's parents for allowing me to write about the work with Davy. Among others I should also like to thank the staff of the service provider 'Link Ability', whose rigorous approach to staff training has made it possible to put in place programmes that have radically altered the quality of damaged people's lives. And many thanks to all those who have contributed thought and time to this work, in particular to Pete Coia for conversations, to Michelle O'Neill for her insight and to Suzanne Zeedyk for her discussion and ideas and for introducing me to the Dundee-Bergen Universities Study Seminars on Child Development and the work we have done together. My editor has been tireless in exploration and prompting and I am deeply grateful to Nicholas Colloff for his eagle eye and red pencil. I also thank Pavilion Publishers for permission to revisit some materials in books previously published by them.

This book amplifies the explorations undertaken in my previous books. It can be seen as a companion volume to *Finding You Finding Me* (Jessica Kingsley Publishers, 2006a), however it can also be profitably read as a stand-alone book. Its argument is drawn from a wider remit than just autism, covering the spectrum of autism and learning disabilities in general. The context in which learning difficulties and autism can be run together is that, whatever the underlying cause, both make it difficult to get in touch – for the individual who experiences them and ourselves who are trying to communicate. Implicit in this are more general questions concerning friendship and relationship. The main thrust is how we can develop emotional engagement with people who are isolated from us by lack of speech. When we establish this meeting ground, what does it do, both for those with whom we share our lives and also for ourselves?

But before we can introduce ourselves to the people who will be our partners on this journey we have to consider what we mean by aspects of communication and intimacy. In Part One we look at the mechanics. Some of the ideas will be familiar to readers of *Finding You Finding Me*, even if presented in a different way. Chapter 1 takes an overall look at the idea of intimacy. Chapter 2 concerns paying attention and the part played in this by eye-contact, and Chapter 3 the particular stresses experienced by people with learning disabilities and with autism. In Chapter 4 we revisit the approach based on the use of a person's own repertoire of behaviours and body language known here in the UK as Intensive Interaction. Chapter 5 asks exactly what it is we are trying to do and Chapter 6 looks at Theory of Mind, an idea that underlies much of current thinking about autism, but which is based on what people on the spectrum are perceived as being unable to do, rather than what they can do if we are able to reduce the level of sensory overload (and consequent stress) they are experiencing. The first half of the book ends with a look at some of the evidence for the effectiveness of the approach known as Intensive Interaction in Chapter 7.

In Part Two of the book, Chapters 8 to 12 describe recent encounters with people with a wide range of disability and age. Although many of the situations described are extreme, it is important to emphasize that the approach adopted does have general applicability. We shall be looking at the place that learning our partner's body language has in relieving their distress and what else we need to do to help them. Chapter 13 explores how the use of a child's body language assists a professional therapist using Sensory Integration to work more effectively. Finally, Chapter 14 assesses a holistic approach which includes all those aspects of our communication partners' lives that are disturbing them and how this state of affairs is altered when we are able to establish a close and intimate relationship with each other.

In all, *From Isolation to Intimacy* is written both for the people I've been lucky enough to teach as well as those they have partnered – and with gratitude for all I have learned from both.

Part One

Learning the Skills of Interaction

1

First Encounters

Intimacy and trust

This book is about relationship, or rather our ability to relate to people who are non-verbal. Most of the individuals whose life stories we shall explore have autism and are at the extreme end of the spectrum. Some, like Jenny, whom we meet first and is blind, and Trish, who has cerebral palsy, simply carry the label, 'learning disability'. To a certain extent the nature of their disability is irrelevant. What they all have in common and what the thrust of this book is about is that in a world that is communication-dependent they cannot talk to us and we cannot talk to them.

('I feel our mutual isolation. We are cut off from each other. You are on your own. How can I talk to you if you cannot tell me who you are?')

Isolation and intimacy: the two poles of affinity. On the one hand we have a state of extreme aloneness, a house in the desert disconnected from everything outside, the track leading to it obliterated by sand, a house that Donna Williams describes as being 'without windows'. Not only is it difficult to find this house – but even if we do, the person inside has her back against the door, has turned in on herself, is in hiding, 'in the corners of her mind...all the relationships she should have with the world outside can only be made in there' (Williams 1999). No allies, no friends, a state of dark introversion.

At the other end of the scale we have intimacy, a condition which has a number of different flavours, from sexual intimacy to the intimacy that we experience with friends. It reflects that they are part of our trusted inner circle with whom we share information that we might not share with others who are not so close to us. The way that intimacy is explored in this book reaches out beyond this. It implies not only closeness but also an ability to put aside self and share one's feelings (emotions) and to enter a mutual playground of the mind.

Yet it is difficult to write about emotion and the sensations that derive from it, since we have no yardstick on which to agree, nothing to measure it by. What I feel may be exaggerated from your point of view, or may seem to you to be my imagination, unless you have also come across the same sensations. And if you do agree with me, I cannot reliably gauge your response against mine. I cannot even rely on my own feelings, since if they are too powerful I may project them on to you – it is you whom I suppose to be upset or angry, when in reality my perception that you are angry derives from my own anger. Feeling is a dangerous maze and easy to get lost in. No wonder that psychologists, in their anxiety to be regarded as scientists, have traditionally avoided navigating the tricky passages of feelings (what they term 'affect'), since they cannot be evaluated objectively. But if we are unwilling to enter and engage with affect we ignore so much of what communication is about. We remain observers, frequently involving ourselves in tortuous explanations, trying to devise rationales and control behaviour without digging deeper into its roots.

Sharing how we feel is not easy. If the language we use to articulate the process of acquiring our insights and mutual affect is colourful and can be described through any of the senses, it is also subjective and non-specific: 'I *see* what you mean', 'I *hear* what you are saying', 'I catch the *flavour* of that', '…get a *whiff*', 'I am *touched* by what you say', 'I *catch* your drift'.

Perhaps the most effective way that I can tell you how I feel (what is going on for me in a way that has meaning for you) is through the use of metaphor, hoping that if this is dynamic enough I shall light a similar spark in your brain. This way you may at least catch a glimpse of my sensory sensation, tap into how I feel. So that if I say, 'my skin crawls', or 'a goose walks over my grave', you do not look for movement – but if it evokes a similar shudder in you, at least you will know what I mean and understand how I feel, be able to put your self alongside and perhaps sympathize with me in my affective plight.

Take intimacy. At present, I am leaning on a gate scribbling down ideas. The foothills of the Dales fold and unfold away towards a white line of snow-capped peaks on the horizon. Every twig and every stone is etched into the landscape by thin winter sunshine. There are drifts of snowdrops, a woodpecker is drilling the long-suffering dead tree in the hedge – and tails wriggling, the first lambs snuggle into their mothers' teats.

Idyllic? Well, not quite. An arctic wind slices my fingers as I struggle to hold the pen. However, in spite of the cold, I should like to be sharing this view with a friend. My guess is that, wrapped up well, we should not talk but stand silent together. All our senses would be dedicated to allowing its crystal beauty to seep through us, sharing the wandering flow of affect, a stream that takes shape from its bed, from the stones over which it sparkles, the light which it captures and the stillness of its pools. Time would slow down to 'this is here, this is now'. Over and above the landscape we should be together. 'Wherever you are, I am, I exist for you.'

But if the nature of intimacy is sharing, the journey on which we are going to embark is no romantic excursion. The practice of intimacy requires self-discipline. We have to learn to discard our defences, to hone all our senses to the presence of other, to hold ourselves in a position of closeness that may at first feel uncomfortable in terms of personal space. In stripping ourselves of our programmes and our own needs and projections, we must orientate ourselves in respect of our partner so that we grow, not just to see their point of view but to look outwards from their condition. We are changed in ways that may be humbling, but we ourselves evolve from the point of our own nakedness.

I should like to put this into a practical context. The other day I visited a house which is lived in by people with very severe learning disabilities. Jenny is blind. She and her support partner are snuggled up together, sharing a giggle about her new bracelet, flat beads which stretch on elastic and snap back, a novel tactile sensation that Jenny has recently been given and is feeling, her short fingers running around each one. Jenny's partner is exploring it with her, but more than that, all her body language is of sharing their affective experience and the fun they are having together. Every movement, every sound she makes, every twitch of her personality is being valued. Through her own bodily responses, Jenny's partner is telling her how much she enjoys being with her. And literally, they are both enjoying themselves as well as each other (not something that it is possible to fake). This may seem a small intervention, but it is the practice of valuing her in this way which has transformed Jenny's life from that of a pattern of withdrawal and distraught self-injury when I first saw her, to the happiness she now evidently experiences. Her carer is also happy. The feedback she is getting is good for her too. She is doing a good job and she knows it. But it is about more than work. It is a living relationship that the two of them have established – and it feels great.

Many of us feel nervous about intimacy, we shrink back, it is too invasive. So let's hold hands and jump in at the deep end. What is it like in here as we surface in this room without defined boundaries, crab-without-a-shell vulnerable to everything, trapped in the ambivalence of a simultaneous desire to hide and reveal? One thing is certain, intimacy is a paradox. This is where we are at our most exposed and yet in a condition of sharing, of naked 'being with'. Invaded by embarrassment, no wonder this can be scary. Trust is the prerequisite – even so, through the nature of our work, we may be being asked to place ourselves in the hands of a person who we do not know and who may also be extremely disturbed and volatile. On the other side, our partner is being asked to trust someone who they do not understand and whose intentions their brain may be interpreting as hostile.

Good intent on its own is not enough. I need to let you know in a way that you can take on board that I am here for you because your cards, your life experience, are stacked against this.

What we have to find is mutuality, a common language, some such demonstrable process by which we can both signal our intent (even if we are not fully conscious of this at the time) and share understanding. We need to be able to see beyond the boundaries of our own blueprints.

Trust addresses our fundamental need for self-preservation. Unless I can develop an attitude of trust, I cannot move out of myself and engage with others. Without it, I shall remain imprisoned in myself, a Flying Dutchman searching for a relationship I cannot attain. I have to believe that when I put myself in your hands, no harm will come to me. In terms of swimming, I have to let go of what is safe and develop an attitude of lying back and floating in what happens, rather than thrashing around trying. I have to trust myself before I can trust you.

Trust is the fertile soil in which we can plant relationship. When we do drop our defences we become accessible to new ideas and experiences, especially in the affective realm. We are touched in a different way. We find that the mark of our partner's personality we feared might bruise us is rather a new horizon offering a fresh landscape, a perspective that engages rather than violates our space. From this standpoint we shall see things differently. Once we get over our fear of proximity, psychological as well as physical, we find that this is where we can meet our partners and learn to know each other, respecting each other's boundaries and valuing each other for the individual people we are. By gaining entrance to 'how' another person feels, confidence grows. We can change their lives and are changed by them.

But before we can gain intimacy, we have to learn how to talk to each other through the language of affect. We are going to learn both to read and use our body language.

> When we talk about body language, we are referring to those features of bodily behaviour which are to some degree under conscious control and which therefore can be used to express different sorts of meaning. The meanings involved are all fairly primitive expressions of attitude or social relationship such as affection, aggression, sexual attraction, greeting, congratulation, gratitude, surprise and the signals of attention. Both tactile and visual modes of communication are employed. (Crystal 2005)

We all use body language, and those of us who have sight monitor that of our communication partners all the time we are speaking to them. But the language David Crystal is talking about in the above extract is intentional, is seen from the point of view of conscious communication. Its expressions are to some extent purposeful, whereas some of the behaviours we shall need to look at simply express how people feel without their intending to do so, through posture or even position. For example, a person backed up against the wall may indicate fear, particularly if we inadvertently raise our arm. When we are with our non-verbal partners, we are going to have to search at a micro-level for every flicker, every movement, every sound and rhythm – and also invest meaning in behaviour we might otherwise reject as just something they do. We are going to have to learn that when our partner licks the wall, scratches their hands or their fingers on the floor, beats the back of their head or tears paper, there is reason for this. Especially, we need to observe how our partner is doing their activity, because it is the 'how' that will tell us how they feel, whether they are content or becoming disturbed. When we give profound attention to other people through body language, we allow ourselves to become vulnerable to their self, very often to the point of intimacy – the closest we can get. We are no longer observers but participants, looking out from our relationship and seeing the world as they see it.

Saying what we mean, meaning what we say

In verbal terms this is what happens if we do not listen: Towards the end of a day's workshop on communication, the speaker invites questions. A man near the back launches into a long rambling description, which is difficult to relate to the content of the course, especially as he does not have a very useful command of language – and speaks with a heavy accent. Eventually the speaker gives up the struggle to understand and turns away. Commenting on this episode later on, a parent says, 'I think he was trying to tell you who he is.'

It is risky to open a book with a personal story, so finding this episode surprisingly shocking, I've used the artificial device of distancing myself by placing it in the third person. Although the error was understandable (the questioner's linguistic disability made him really difficult to understand and at the end of a tiring day my mind was half-wandering to the long, dark drive home), it highlights so clearly the fundamental difficulty that we face when we try to talk to each other, the gulf that can exist between the words we use and the underlying intent of the communication. Pete Coia, a clinical psychologist, puts this succinctly when he suggests that so often we listen and respond to 'form rather than the message' (personal communication), the container rather than the content. In doing this we focus on what a person is saying, rather than the underlying intrinsic reality of what they are trying to say. And in addition to the speaker's mislaid intent, their listener can misinterpret their message in the light of her own distraction. So easily we find ourselves holding the wrong end of the stick.

In trying to tell me that when he actually asked people for help they were always able to give him the assistance he needed, the questioner had missed the point of the discussion, which was that there are some people who cannot ask for help, either because they are unable to do so, or because their conversation partner is not listening. But my need as speaker was to get over to the audience the difficulties experienced by some people with disability. However, in pursuing my own agenda, I had totally missed what the questioner needed to tell me, that is about his own life and experience. The fact that his interjection was inappropriate at this time is irrelevant. In failing to listen to the inner message of what he was saying (although I had heard the sound of his words and had continued to struggle with the content of these), I had not listened to his need and so had failed to confirm him as a person. Had I realised, I could have suggested we met afterwards and talked. As it was, in any meaningful sense we had passed each other by. I was left baffled and he was left rejected. We had lost the chance to communicate with each other in any real sense.

Looking at the whole person

From Isolation to Intimacy is an exploration of how, if we learn to read and use a person's own body language, we can establish contact with them. It explores how this fits into the whole business of improving the quality of life of people who in one way or another are isolated by their disability. In trying to unravel some of the more tangled psychological and behavioural situations with which we may find ourselves confronted, it becomes clear that positive outcomes are not just about using body language but putting this in context, understanding what it does and does not do and responding to the whole ecology of our partner. Working with people who have very severe complex needs, we need to look at everything this person is experiencing. We need to know how they are processing or failing to process the sensory information that comes to them, since this is the filter through which they get to know what is going on round them and how it will affect them. In so many cases it is not failure to hear, see and feel, but the failure to process adequately the sensations we derive from our sensory intake, that underpins distressed and difficult behaviour. For example, a stimulus that is benign in intent may be misinterpreted as threatening. We cannot consider one aspect of a person in isolation but need to look at all the factors that affect their lives.

What are the limits of using non-verbal body language? Is it exclusive? Does it stand on its own or is it part of a holistic way of interaction, a way that encompasses the whole dynamic of a person's activities and responses, an ecosystem which has to include the inner world of motivation – not just of those with whom we try to connect, but also our own?

Listening to how people say they feel

The failure of the capacity to relate comes in many forms. It can be that the ability to connect is muffled by damage to the sensory organs, as in blindness or deafness. For example, a person with tunnel vision sees the world through a tube. The absence of peripheral vision means they have no advance warning of people coming up from the side. Their brains may interpret such events as hostile because they have had no time to prepare so they respond with aggression. We need to let them know we are coming before we move. Or a person may be psychologically hobbled, unable to reach out beyond the boundaries set by their own blueprints. In the case of autism (although a person who is on the spectrum may also be blind) the sensory organs are usually working but, for whatever reason, the processing of information is out of sync with the intake. People on the autistic spectrum who are able will say that their understanding drops in and out; sometimes they know what is going on round them and sometimes they do not have a clue. What are we to understand when a child says that his brain plays tricks on him? What does he mean? What does he feel?

Some of the images we have from people with autism are extremely vivid, such as the sensation described by a child as like 'a whole load of spiders trying to crawl out of my skin'. Those of us who have never experienced this do not have to go through an intermediate visual processing stage but recoil immediately, knowing inside ourselves how it might feel and trying to distance ourselves from such a powerful description.

Periodically Micky says that his head is 'switched off', and sometimes he will come and say, 'Switch my head on please.' His father says that the correct response is to extend the wrist and rotate it – as in turning a switch – and that sometimes this is effective in helping his son to reconnect. He continues the conversation in the same language, the language of the metaphor which his son used. But the picture he draws vividly illustrates for me a sensation that is not a part of my life experience, a period when the brain stops processing, goes blank, just as the light goes off when I depress the switch, disconnecting the bulb from its electricity. In a similar fashion, Jim complains he has got 'his silly head on' but he manages to regulate this condition on his own by announcing he is going to 'switch back over' and making a visual switch sign himself. When their brains are incoherent, both Micky and Jim respond to input in another mode, even if Micky needs someone else to do it for him. This does suggest that if a person's cognitive faculties are scrambled, the most effective interventions to put them back on track may be transmitting the confirmatory message they require in an alternative mode to speech.

To look at this from another angle, if Micky and Jim's confusion is the outcome of failure to process, how is it that they know this is so – and perhaps more pertinently, who are the Micky and Jim who know their brains are not working, because from my point of view, these are the young boys I want to meet.

If we want to understand people, we need to listen to what they are saying, to what they are trying to tell us. In order to enter into their world, we need to accept their metaphor in our flesh, embody it, so we feel what they feel and begin to see the world from their point of view.

As I said, *From Isolation to Intimacy* covers a whole range of individuals, from those with multiple disability, through severe disability to those with distressed and difficult-to-manage behaviour, some of whom are on the autistic spectrum. It not only pays attention to those who do not speak but also to some who are on the borderlines of speech or who are using it, but not in such a way as to communicate who they are. It asks and tries to answer what can be done to get in touch with those whose lack of ability to tell us about themselves and what they want either has a physical cause or is because they have withdrawn into an inner world.

A conversation with Ron

Ron is non-verbal but extremely vocal. He has come with his parents to a training day on communication, since he has been excluded from a number of schools that cannot cope with his behaviour. He is sitting at the back of the hall in a wheelchair. The situation is not a good one for him because he does not care for contact with people and here he is in a hall with about 30 parents. He wears his baseball cap pulled firmly down over his eyes, hiding behind it and making loud noises to the extent that it is becoming difficult to make myself heard. It occurs to me that instead of talking about a way of interacting, it would be more effective to show people what I mean. So I begin to respond. Each time he makes a sound I answer with a related sound or rhythm. Almost at once Ron starts to listen and our reciprocal interaction becomes a conversation. He raises his head – and the peak of his cap so that he can attend more fully. Everyone is watching him as he becomes more interested and pushes the peak round

to the side and then back to front so that he can see better. His face is
gleeful. Out of his sensory chaos, here is something which has meaning
for him and to which he can respond. A channel has been opened for us to
talk to each other – and it is clear he has a lot to say.

Who is talking to whom?

To some extent we are all refugees wandering a world of conflict
searching for the homeland of knowing who we are. We endlessly look
for the confirmation that we exist. And when we do not listen to the inner
messages of others, we deny our partners in communication the
confirmation they need. So if I want to meet you, where do I look?

When I recall a friend, I may have a picture in mind; but as well as this,
I also have a qualitative memory, how they feel to me. If I try and describe
her to you, I might say she is tall and has fair hair and blue eyes – but all
this will tell you is her physical type and nothing about her as a personality. For that I shall have to go beyond her physique to try and convey why
she is special to me. And each of us is different, we have our own special
mix of nature and nurture, our flavour, what one might call our own
affective signature. This is important, because it is here we are going to
have to direct our attention if we want to relate to each other, focusing on
this essence, this core.

Most of the time we live inside the cardboard box of our own experience. We see things from our own point of view, rarely lifting the lid even
when we are in the company of others. In an ideal communication it is me
thinking about you and what you say, talking to you – and you are
listening to me and thinking about what I say and answering and I am
responding to you. In reality it is usually both an internal and an external
process, involving exchange not only between two parties (or rather
partners as I shall refer to them) but including the internal processing of
each – which is where our interaction can get lost. Both of us can be
paying attention to each other, engaged with and responding to what the
other says, but in practice it is rarely so simple, because each of us is
directed to a greater or lesser degree by the blueprints and feelings of our
inner world. Information received is processed and responses are shaped
in the light of our own experience, experiences of which our partner may
not be aware, nor might we be in a conscious sense. Although this mixed
bag can be beneficial, in that we introduce each other to experience and

points of view which are new to us, it can also be totally misleading for both parties if the internal agendas are in charge, directing the interaction into the cul-de-sac of personal need. If we really listen to people, we begin to see not just a different point of view but also that even their starting point may be a new one for us.

So often in conversation we just cruise along, not thinking about the person to whom we speak as a person. The following story highlights the difference between a superficial exchange that is intended as a pleasantry and an interaction focusing on a person's inner world.

Conversation with Nick

Nick is in his sixties but seems older, is grizzled and has retreated into himself. He makes no attempt to interact unless he feels there is a possibility that such an encounter will lead to something to eat. He is on the autistic spectrum and has frequent aggressive and destructive outbursts. He either stays in his room or wanders about lost in repetitive behaviours, for example, flicking switches. In a world that he experiences as sensory chaos, when he goes through these rituals he knows what he is doing. How he feels is reflected in the way he performs these activities, which become increasingly agitated as his stress level rises. Attempts to join in his repetitive behaviours seem to irritate him, and his disturbed behaviour escalates.

When we meet he is wearing a festive paper hat with a broad brim pulled down over his eyes, which he adjusts occasionally, either to get a better view or to hide from what is going on. He is not having a good morning and his support partner warns he is on the verge of an outburst. In addition to his change in body and facial language, Nick is now making sounds which are becoming louder and express increasing upset. In order to reduce the pressure on him we retreat to the passage outside his flat. Once there, I start to respond to each sound as he makes it, not necessarily using the same sound but a related one, one that is close enough for him to feel is meaningful and which in terms of affect, empathizes with his previous sound. He can hear me but not see me, so there is less processing for his brain, it is less confusing for him. After a while he comes out and sits in a chair in the passage. As soon as he realizes that each sound he makes will always get an answer, the ones he is making soften. His support partner joins in and we respond quietly, until we are all three engaged in empathetic exchange. He is acutely attentive, as are we. At this stage he starts to wriggle his foot and watches to see if we will wriggle ours.

As the pace of our interaction slows and our engagement leads to a triad of intimacy, even the background noise of the restless ongoing conversation with our own internal senses is suspended in the presence of 'flow'. Such intimacy has nothing to do with sexuality but is a quality of total regard, an intimate attention to the affect of other (how they feel), where all the senses are tuned in to awareness of other.

At this point, a passing support worker comes through a swing door. She is not aware of what is going on and breaks in loudly and cheerfully with a comment about Nick's hat, teasing him about its incongruity, saying he 'looks ridiculous in it'. In the context of our total mutual attention, the effect of this unintentional but nevertheless bulldozing insensitivity is one of shock, even of momentary outrage. Her interruption feels as if a cricket ball had splintered the glass bubble of a precious relationship. However, our instinctive reaction to this highlights for me the difference between an exterior conversation, which is rooted in what we perceive from our own sensory experience, and the inward conversation of 'self with other', the focus of which is shifted to an exploration of our partner's experience. While the commentator's visual perception of a man in a silly and inappropriate hat was correct, she had missed the general tenor and importance of the conversation she interrupted. It was taking place on a completely different plane. What we were engaged in was the first step in a delicate process of establishing contact and building a framework of trust with a man whose life can only be described as a wreck.

What do we mean by communication?

Working this way, our perception of what is meant by communication changes. In this particular interaction with Nick there were three of us. We were all totally absorbed in our experience of other. Not having come across this quality of interaction previously, Nick's communication partner commented how moving it had been. A similar remark was made to me by a young key worker following a communication session: 'I did not know it could be like this.' Exchange of affect, putting our selves alongside people, begins to take priority over exchange of information.

In a personal communication Michelle O'Neil wrestles with this changing attitude in herself:

> I think that if we are to develop communication and break through communication barriers, we must open our hearts and minds and allow ourselves to be led into what the world means for others. I suppose it's about taking yourself into someone else's territory and whilst remaining as yourself, having the flexibility to allow yourself to grow and move with the person you are communicating with. I feel I am only just beginning to understand what communication has the capacity to be about. It's daunting and exhilarating at the same time.

In Denmark, Inge Rødbroe uses body language to work with deaf-blind children. Nafstad and Rødbroe (1999) describe an absolute need to subject oneself to the deaf-blind child's needs. We have to learn to put aside our own needs and expectations in favour of those of our partner, so that our perception moves in concert with their affective state. In practising communication we never take our L-plates off. Each time there is this sense of being a beginner, of a novice embarking on an adventure.

Can we communicate without speech?

Where a person cannot speak, it is all too easy to assume that he or she has nothing to tell us. The problem is put very simply, blue letters on a white lapel button given to me: 'Not being able to speak is not the same as not having anything to say.' Unfortunately, it is all too easy to overlook this distinction, based on an assumption that the person is passive because 'this is how he or she is'. Because the person cannot articulate what he or she wants, we overlook his or her experience in favour of our own. We assume, quite wrongly in many cases, that our partner's needs and feelings are the same as ours because we have no other guidelines than our own interpretation of our partner's response or lack of interest.

For example, eye-contact is very important to us, and I am told that Richard loves to look into people's eyes. And yet when one is the subject of this it has a very peculiar feel to it, and one realizes that rather than 'looking into', he is 'staring at'. When we look at something we are showing interest, so we assume others are doing the same. We judge others by ourselves. But there is a difference between 'stare' and 'gaze' (marked by the childhood admonishment, 'Don't stare, it's rude', presumably because the rather odd phenomenon of 'staring down' is associated with establishing a place in the pecking order). In a rigid, fixated stare the person appears to be looking for himself or herself, whereas in a gaze the person is opening up to 'other than self'. To be stared at is to come up against a blank wall with no intention or possibility of exchange.

It is easy to be mistaken if we judge others by ourselves. Even with the adoption of such approaches as Advocacy and Person Centred Planning, it is very difficult for us to see into the worlds of non-verbal people who cannot tell us about themselves, to understand their world from a point of view uncontaminated by our own.

Or is it? To answer this question we need to stand back and take a look at what we mean by communication.

Functional communication and emotional engagement

On the one hand we have the standard definition of communication found in the *Oxford English Dictionary*, which talks about exchange of information through speech, words, reading and so on. However, robots and machines can exchange information. But human beings are social animals. In order to get to really know each other we want to reach deeper than *functional communication*, the level of, 'I want a cup of tea.' As well as information we want *emotional engagement* with each other. We want to know how other people feel and we want them to know how we feel. George Vaillant, professor of psychiatry at Harvard University puts this powerfully: 'I wish to remind the reader that we have limbic systems as well as cerebral cortices and that the brain cannot be separated from the heart' (Vaillant 1993). As well as being physically dependent on each other we need to be able to attune ourselves to others, to empathize and be alongside them.

When I was at school I was puzzled by the distinction between sympathy and empathy. Now that I have learned that sympathy is an attitude that requires a conscious effort to align myself to – 'I am sorry you are feeling sad' – I am still at a loss to know how empathy – 'I feel your sadness' – actually happens. How is it that your affect moves through me, I sense it in my flesh? Is it simply that, working off subliminal clues I internalize my understanding in an outside-in process, or is it rather as it appears to be, direct transmission that starts from the inside and works out?

At a conference on Intensive Interaction in Leeds in 2006 the discussion turned towards communication, not just as information exchange, 'functional communication', but recognizing the need to explore the emotional element of our interactions – the 'getting-close-to-you' component. I want to pause a minute to think about what emotional engagement actually involves.

It is easy to draw up a list of the emotions – anger, fear, sadness, joy, and so on – but such a taxonomy misses the point of engagement. We are so hardened that the language we need to use when trying to articulate the world of self and other is in danger of sounding 'over-the-top'. It is too tender, too raw, too naked, too precious. How can we turn ourselves inside out so that our inner world, the place where we feel, connects with the sentient space of our partner?

Imagine yourself to be a leather glove with a soft lining. The leather skin protects the vulnerable under-layer from the world about it. Turn yourself inside out. Now you are exposed, undefended but also – and perhaps because of this – extremely aware of your partner, you find yourself hypersensitive to their affect. A young practitioner said, 'It's like we are dipping into the heart and soul of our partner' (Michelle O'Neill, personal communication). Our use of affective language is so debased that it may be hard to capture the immense simplicity of this statement. Stripped down it points to and arrives at exactly the place where we need to be. And the verb 'dipping' is important. We do not belly-flop into our partner's world but, ideally and with profound respect for their responses, we try to slide in without causing a ripple, so that we do not trigger our partner's anxiety.

How often do we meet someone by walking into their room, an unknown stranger and greeting them in our language? When I am working with someone who is very disturbed, I wait outside their door until I have picked up enough of what they are doing to introduce myself in their language, using their sounds or rhythms, in effect saying, 'Hello, here I am' in such a way as tells them I am not going to do anything that they will perceive as threatening.

On the other hand it is very easy to think of empathy as a nice warm feeling of togetherness, a pleasant mutual buzz of oxytocin, when in practice laying ourselves open to people's feelings, especially their negative ones, may be extremely uncomfortable and carry us beyond our commonly accepted social boundaries.

If someone says to us 'I want to hit you', and their fist is screwed up and tense so we know they mean it, or shouts 'Fuck off', these are indications of separation and distress. Instead of rejecting such negative behaviour in one way or another, we need to reach into the sensation that is triggering this and confirm it in a way that lets our partners know that we really are alongside them. Seeing the world through their eyes we feel what they feel. So we say, 'You must feel like hitting me' or 'You sound really fucked off.' This respects how our partners feel and says yes, we stand with them and share their anger and distress, even if it is directed towards us. We acknowledge and confirm their feeling instead of denying it. (By denying it we say their feeling is not real and so deny the validity of themselves. We also deny them a pattern of reference for identifying other people's feelings since we learn about the feelings of others by correctly identifying them with our own.) If we are prepared to open ourselves in a way that allows them to know that we know and accept how they feel (and at the same time maintain our own integrity) there is always a palpable change in the quality of the engagement showing itself as a shift from anger to relief ('someone has taken the lid off my distress and seen how it is for me'). At this stage our partner will almost always physically turn towards us and say quite simply, 'Yes, I do' (want to hit you) or 'Yes, I am' (fucked off) and they relax. An interaction which had become rigid and polarized has regained its flexibility and we can move on together.

However, the relevance of this particular excursion is not so much an enquiry as to how we should react to aggression but rather to point out that emotional engagement can be a bumpy ride. We have all been sworn at, and I have already addressed the problem of swearing in my book *Finding You Finding Me*. But briefly, what is it that is so taboo about the F-word, that when it is articulated during a discussion on swearing to an audience of emotionally literate professional communicators, it draws a mini shock-wave expressed in the form of a collective gasp? As a colleague pointed out it is only a word – but nevertheless a combination of four letters so arresting that the brain instantly rearranges them, even when mis-spelt on a T-shirt.

The problem with being at the receiving end of this word is that it expresses not only the amazing thing we do with and give our partners within a loving relationship – but when it is used in a vituperative sense rather than simply as part of a low-level reiterant effing, it represents the ultimate violence against another person, an expression of power where it treats them like an object, a thing. In rejecting their humanity, the affect it carries is not only that of disconnection but also the aggression of the perpetrator and the fear of the victim. In the context of empathizing with our partners, to turn towards and engage with such feeling is to be dragged by the scruff of the neck into our partner's despair.

So when I am confronted with such extremes, should I run for cover (psychologically if not physically) or should I engage, enter, feel, express how it feels and truly value my partner's feeling and in so doing validate them as a person? Putting aside my timidity and inhibition seems a small price to ease my partner's sense of aloneness and to help them know who they are.

And in so doing, we find ourselves getting real – in a way that adds colour and reassurance to the lives of both of us. We move into the dimension of trust, we feel supported and know where we are with each other. 'Our very survival and development depend on our capacity to recruit the invested interest of others' (Keagan 1982).

So how can we find out how a person feels if they can't tell us?

2

Attention

Eye-contact

Attention is a two-way process: me focusing on you and you focusing on me. Unfortunately we read the body language of others through the spectacles of our own experience. I am surprised when a child with no sight rolls over on her back, turning her face away from me as I echo her non-verbal sounds with taps; that is until I recognize that there is something about the tilt of her head which suggests she is presenting her 'best ear' so that she can hear me. Her subsequent smiles confirm that she is listening carefully. Even where the primary sense (most often, vision) is common to both partners, it is very easy to find ourselves interpreting the same situation differently, especially where one partner is on the autistic spectrum.

For those of us who have sight, three quarters of our sensory intake is visual and eye-contact is taken as a measure of the degree of attention and often as synonymous with it. Those of us not on the spectrum feel discomforted if our partners avoid eye-contact and in many situations believe they are not 'listening' to us. In addition, this inability of ours to read the response of our partner may make it difficult for us to ask a delicate question over the phone, a situation where we cannot monitor and read the response in a person's eyes. We need to see how they react, even if only through a swift glance. This gives us permission to move on, perhaps to probe more deeply, or tells us we are on dangerous territory and need to withdraw. (Also, how can I know if you are telling me the truth and are sincere, if I cannot see your eyes?) When the teacher says to a child, 'Look at me', it is not just a physical reorientation that she desires. What she actually means is, 'Transfer your attention from your inner world to me and to what I am saying (that is, the world outside yourself) so that I can see if you are taking it on board.'

However, as already pointed out, if I look at you I not only see the colour of your hair and eyes, the shape of your face and what you are wearing, I notice how you feel, and also how you feel about me, where we stand in relation to each other, a crucial skill in the art of making friends and allies. Yet although in conversation even those of us who are neurotypical do not look at people all the time, we do constantly refer back to them, letting them know through quick glances how we feel about what they are saying. Apart from our feeling of frustration at not being certain if our partner is taking on board the information we are trying to give them, it is the absence of emotional content that makes connection feel uneasy with people who avoid eye-contact. This leads to our talking glibly about eye-contact as an end in itself, as if it were the only criterion for attention and engagement.

Psychologists favour eye-contact since it is easy to record and is seen as giving an objective measurement of the degree of engagement. But for all of us, eye-contact is not just a negative or a positive – the reality is a scale which dips and rises through the whole hierarchy of intimacy, from 'glare' (definitely hostile), 'stare' (which treats the recipient as an object), via 'look' (which may be interested or uninterested) to gaze, the cusp of which is a state which is known as dyadic, where partners wander in each other's presence. When we think of 'drowning' in another's gaze, what we seem to be saying is that all our senses are subsumed into total awareness of other and (at the same time) self. We are no longer aware of individual sensations; we simply 'become attention', lost in affective flow, blind to the world outside. Lovers are aware of the eye's caress, a visual exchange of deep emotional significance. In gaze, whether it be with the beloved, or simply that we are entranced by the invitation to enter into the world of another, all the barriers of fear and inhibition come tumbling down. This is not just eye-contact, this is the dyadic communion which is so powerful that it is the onlooker who is discomforted, feeling they are intruders. And when using the body language of another, this empathic flow is not just the prerogative of neurotypicals but can be experienced between autistic partners – and between autistic and non-autistic partners, given favourable conditions. For example, when making the training film *Learning the Language* with Gabriel, a young man with very severe autism and learning disabilities, we moved in four hours from a position where he was treating me with the same indifference as he would a lump of furniture, to one of such intimacy that it elicited the comment, 'How can she get that close?' from a witness. But under such circumstances this is not uncommon. Our desire to meet each other is mutual.

What is so difficult for those of us not on the spectrum to be aware of is that people with autism who are avoiding eye-contact do so because their responses to sensory overload and the consequent feedback they receive from their own nervous systems can be acute confusion or pain, rather than manageable factual or emotional information. For a person with autism, the demand to 'Look at me' is like forcing the door, breaking into their house and expecting the owner to welcome us with a cup of tea. As Therese Jolliffe points out (Jolliffe *et al.* 1992), people are especially difficult since the sensory picture they present is one of constantly changing shape, sounds and demands, all of which have to be processed and interpreted. Donna Williams explains the effect that eye-contact can have on her as a person with autism:

> For example, when I was impacted upon by eye-contact with others, this sometimes resulted in my punching myself sharply…the emotional impact of this eye-contact gripped my stomach with such intensity and suddenness that I felt the 'looker' had punched me by this crime of looking at me. (Williams 2006)

Donna goes on to explain that in her case she felt she was being attacked and that by hitting herself she was showing her 'attacker' what they were doing to her. As a neurotypical person, I need to remember that I may pose a threat simply by my presence and that demanding eye-contact is not the best way of claiming attention.

And yet there is a considerable sweep in the range of unpleasant and painful sensory feedback experienced even within the autistic spectrum. At a conference, delegates on the spectrum may say they are 'peopled out' and retire to their rooms for a while to recover. And yet such over-stimulation differs only in degree from my own when I get to the stage that I simply cannot cope with information overload. My brain switches off and I go for a walk. On the other hand, I may deliberately downcast my eyes if I am discussing a subject of deep import and wish to listen to what is being said in itself, rather than its being coloured by contingent visual messages. But this is completely different from those others on the spectrum who have been unable to equip themselves with the protective devices of the less vulnerable and who are thrown into sometimes severe pain by any sort of eye-contact, or who have learned to totally withdraw to the point where they tell us that they do not know what people are for.

So what do we miss if we avoid eyeball to eyeball contact? It's not just the eyes – how wide the pupils are – but all the myriad muscle movements immediately surrounding the eyes that widen, deepen, conceal and sharpen our messages. Some emotional messages, known as micro-facial expressions may be extremely swift (as short as one twenty fifth of a second) so that unless we are particularly on the lookout we are going to miss them, or only observe them subliminally. Of course, we can pick up a great deal of information by observing body language generally, but what eye-contact does for those of us who can bear it is to fine-tune an interaction in terms of the flow of affect.

And since very little in human terms is black or white, in terms of eye-contact there is an autistic/neurotypical continuum which, at one end is able to obtain and make use of the affective information it gains from eye-contact and at the other can be intrusive and painful. All of us, whether autistic or not, move backwards and forwards along the continuum depending on the degree of intimacy we can manage, or seems appropriate at the time. While the more able (or less threatened) can learn to look at part of the face, the chin or nose rather than the eyes (and some may suggest this is because they present less information than the eyes), those more vulnerable to the pain of emotional feedback may simply cut out completely. What does irritate some people on the spectrum is the neurotypical assumption that if they are not looking they are not attending.

Although perhaps it is possible to imagine two wine-tasters mutually abandoned in contemplation of a great vintage, or two chefs jointly savouring an especially delectable ingredient, it is more usual to lose oneself in affective flow through vision, hearing or touch. What is at stake is the quality of dedication and the ability to fine-tune to attention, be the experience solitary or shared.

The point of this somewhat roundabout diversion is that, if I am to have any hope of meeting my partner, I need to learn to attend not only to his or her sensory experience but also to how he or she receives my sensory messages. I do this by setting aside my own world and entering my partner's, to focus not just with my eyes or ears, how I feel or see or hear – but with all my senses.

Paying attention

Suppose I want to hear the proverbial pin drop. From my surroundings I shall require quietness so there is no auditory competition but also stillness, so that my visual sense is undisturbed, since even if I am listening, my attention can be distracted by input in another mode. As well, I shall need proximity, close enough so that I am physically in a position to apprehend the minute echoes of impact.

But as well as freedom from external distraction, I shall also need consciously to dedicate all my attention to whoever or whatever is my objective. In order to clarify this I want to look at it from a completely different angle.

Walking along the South-East Kent coast, one is surprised to come across what appear to be gigantic concrete ash trays tipped on one side. Constructed towards the end of the First World War, the purpose of these pre-radar dishes was to pick up the faint throb of approaching zeppelins, giving aeroplanes time to scramble and destroy the invader before they reached the shore. In themselves, these defensive ears are neutral, relaying any sound, baaing sheep, revving trial bikes or passing lorries: it is the observer's attention that shifts 'hearing' to 'listening and discernment'. During recent televised trials to see if the system still worked after so many years, it was clear that the microphone needed to be extremely accurately placed in order to pick up the relayed incoming message of an advancing plane. Again and again the technician tracked round and round, up and down, backwards and forwards, putting everything else aside as he homed in on the exact focal point, all his senses channelled to locating optimum reception. In terms of body language, everything about him was dedicated to this end so that to an observer, he seemed to merge with and became part of that end, so closely attuned that he became one with his objective.

But in itself this may not be enough. In addition to the quality of our focus we need to be sure where it is that our partner's attention is focused, exactly what it is that they are interested in. For example, it is easy to focus on (and be distracted by) a gross movement or activity, what first strikes us about our partners, rather than the minutiae of what it is that has meaning for them.

Robert, who is in his thirties, loves to play with toy cars, so in an effort to join in with his activity I get some of my own and play with them alongside him – but he takes no notice of my efforts. When I look a bit more closely, he is holding his cars a few inches from his face and turning them very slowly backwards and forwards, peering through at the light. Adjusting my movements to his, exploring in my own senses what he is getting out of his activity, I find that he is lining up the windows on the driver and passenger sides of his toy so that when he looks through at the light he aligns a sight, a very small frame in which to hold his swirling kaleidoscope vision. Far from being age-inappropriate, this is not a game as we know it but the serious business of freeze-framing an otherwise elusive sensory experience. We are in danger of getting it all wrong if we do not fine-tune our attention to the sensory experience of our partners. Where is it they are zeroing in?

Since they are prevented from communicating with us and the world outside, what is it that our partners are looking for in themselves? In her profound exploration of her own autism, Donna Williams introduces us to her two worlds. She talks about 'my world' (an 'inside world') and 'the world' (the 'outside world'), the world out there, roughly inside the fortress and outside its walls (Williams 1999).

Although Donna has autistic spectrum disorder, the inner–outer-world mindset is not confined to people on the spectrum. But I want to define more clearly the specific model she is talking about here, since there is room for confusion. Fortunately she gives us a extraordinarily clear picture in her documentary *Jam Jar*, which opens with her poem, 'Nobody Nowhere', followed by an elucidation of its meaning.

What we learn from her courageous exposition is that the 'inside world' is a refuge from overwhelming sensory confusion and the negative responses of the outer world:

> When it's all turmoil out there, there's no turmoil in there.

> A state of total withdrawal into yourself where the whole world is replaced and made redundant and you have every relationship with yourself that you could have had with the people in the world and they don't matter any more.

> Everything outside is redundant, all replaced and all self-contained to the point where it doesn't matter and there is no sense of where or sense of who, there just is.

> When you are that self-contained you don't see out any more. (Williams 1995)

In fact attention is totally directed inwards, in the case of autism on some inward bodily sensation or a sensation hijacked from the outside world and used as the object of self-stimulus.

So Donna does not seem to be talking about the concept of the conscious and unconscious mind so much as about the direction in which her attention is directed and the degree of concentration (in order to avoid the unpleasant and painful affects of over-stimulation). And we are all protective of an inner world, the internal world of dreams and the fretful half-lit world of perceptions on the borders of consciousness: part memories of actions and part memories of feelings with their contingent fantasies, the fiction and non-fiction stories of our lives. Some of this we call daydreaming, and according to our make-up we give it more or less attention. Most of us will have experienced at some stage of our lives a state where we become lost in our reverie. Interruptions will jerk us out of our self-mesmerizing state – but this is accompanied by a sensation of change, that we have been somewhere else. At least we can maintain the freedom to come and go, dip in and out of the inner world where every-thing just is – but as Donna Williams points out, there is a difference: 'You can visit in freedom – but if you are compelled to live in this state you live in fear.' This fear is the outcome of not knowing what will happen because of sensory confusion, which Therese Jolliffe describes as terror that something dreadful may occur (particularly the confusion and pain of fragmentation when the brain ceases to function).

However, there is also a different way in which we can be said to be talking to ourselves. All of us are involved in an ongoing neural brain–body conversation. The brain is sending messages to the body telling the various parts of it what to do. The body sends feedback to the brain saying that it has done whatever it is. Whether or not we are aware of it, this brain–body dialogue is going on all the time. The most obvious example of this is in the conversation between the brain and the lungs. Highly simplified, the brain says 'breath in', and the body sends a return message telling the brain that it has 'done it'. Should this process fail we should die. Although we are not conscious of this rhythmic exchange unless we are panting from exertion, or are deliberately focusing on it as in some forms of meditation, people who have withdrawn into their inner world may be listening exclusively to the feedback they are receiving from their own body rhythms (especially those who have severe learning disabilities or are on the autistic spectrum). If we are going to get in touch with such individuals it is crucial that we realize that at its most extreme, this means they may be listening to the soft sounds of inhalation and exhalation to the exclusion of everything else which is going on in the world outside. Like a snail, they are totally withdrawn inside the shell of their inner world. Even more, like a vortex all their attention is spiralled into their inner world.

In the previous chapter we met Ron and Nick. We saw that by paying attention to and using their body language (the way that they are talking to themselves) we could draw their interest from an inner world to engagement with ourselves. Ron physically signalled his fascination by shifting his cap round so that he could see the source of the stimulus that so beguiled him, and eventually took it off altogether, something his parents had never seen before under similar circumstances.

Nick moved himself from his sitting room to join us in the passage outside, but he also moved from a seriously disturbed state to one of tranquillity, where he was relaxed and enjoying a naturally flowing interaction. We who were working with him also moved from a position of nervous anticipation of his reputation to mutual trust. His support partner was amazed and said he had never experienced this degree of closeness with him before.

So by our paying attention to what it is that has significance and meaning for our partners, we shift their focus of interest from solitary self-stimulus to shared activity. In practice it is not difficult to see this redirection of attention from inner to outer world, from self-stimulation to desire to communicate, from hibernation to alertness. From a situation where they are 'cut off', 'switched off', our partners begin to smile, to be interested in what we are doing and to respond by altering their body posture. As far as possible, they orientate themselves towards us, referring back and bringing in new initiatives to see how we will respond. They become lively and alert – 'switched on' – and may come closer to us. Through changes in their body language we perceive their reorientation, even though the clues may be so small as to be almost subliminal. At the same time we begin to have more of a sense of how they feel, we see a new side to them, they become real to us, friends who we care about in a different and personal way, however good our practice before.

Now our partners have two states of attention. The first is to their inner world where the individual is totally self-absorbed. In the second, attention is directed outwards. Working with a small boy called Davy suggests there is a third. Although deeply withdrawn into his inner world, there are times when he seems to be listening attentively to something that has caught his attention from the world outside, as when he plays on the swing. During this time he is completely absorbed in the sensation offered by the massive jolt he receives each time the swing alters direction. I stop the swing and move it extremely gently and slowly from side to side instead of backwards and forwards. This is a new vestibular sensation and he really homes in on it. He appears to be thinking very hard indeed with his whole body, everything orientated and attentive to this novel feeling, listening to his own reaction rather than being swallowed by it. Although he is not referring back to me to see what I think, he is giving total attention to some event which his brain recognizes as new but significant to him, and one that is instigated outside himself.

But at this stage our neat categorization starts to break down, the boundaries become blurred. What about the child who is opening and shutting doors, tearing paper, demanding to watch the same video over and over again. Is she not interested in something outside herself? Or is it that she is, as Robert was with his cars, hijacking some source of self-stimulation from the outside world and using it to feed their inner world with a particular sensation, so that by a process of continuous refocus she keeps sensory over-stimulation at bay and maintains coherence. This certainly looks different from attention to what is named by psychologists as the third object, when there is interest in the object for its own sake.

An alternative situation is where our partner feels so vulnerable that in order to hide the overwhelming feedback from their emotional state, they project their feeling into this third object or person. In such a situation our partner may initiate a false persona or personas (see Chapter 12). In this case it may be extremely difficult to tell quite where the individual's attention is focused, since although their voice or voices sound detached, they are sometimes a very efficient shield, masking the 'vulnerable person'. If we listen carefully, we may detect something pseudo, wooden or unreal in the tone of their communication; it doesn't sound part of the actual person. (It seems probable that in this case, the location of their attention is in maintenance of their often elaborate defence system.)

Finding our partner's self

To return to Ron and Nick. Before I could make contact with them I had to suspend all sensory distractions and particularly, I had to stop listening to my own internal conversation ('How can I make contact with him?', 'Can I get this right?', 'I'll look silly in front of everyone if this doesn't work', and in Nick's case, 'Am I going to get hit?'). I had to put aside everything round me and switch to watching and listening, tuning in with all my senses. I needed a radical redirection from self to the question of 'What is important to him?' That is, where is his attention focused? What gives him his sense of being? Because this is where I needed to feed myself in.

In each partnership, the focal point we need to locate is the point at which our partner feels themselves to be, the physical location of where they get their sense of self. As I have sought to explain in *Finding You Finding Me*, in order to locate this place we have to look for exactly where it is that our partner is physically giving themselves sensory stimulus, how they are talking to themselves. Furthermore, we need to fine-tune on the affective content, the feeling quality, that these actions express, by observing not just what they are doing but also how their sounds or movements are done. It is sensitivity to the *how* of their body language that will give us access to the emotional world of a partner and their current disposition – how they are feeling at this minute. As was pointed out in the previous chapter, for Nick, tuning into his 'arranging mode' seemed to increase his agitation. The most easily identifiable index of his stress level was the rise in audibility and pitch of his sounds – this was an expression of how he felt. His body language indicated he was clearly very stressed and about to blow at any minute.

Although it is perfectly possible to work with a partner's movements (see using Gabriel's flicking movements in the training video *Learning the Language*), in practice, working with their sounds is the easiest way to communicate, not least as it can be done at a distance. This was particularly so with Ron who, while he responded brilliantly when we were at opposite ends of the hall, felt too crowded when I moved nearer. From cheerful communication, he closed down again. His cap came back round and he pulled the peak down again. Immediate proximity overloaded him, and for him the condition for interaction was distance. Or, as when we were working with Nick, using sound at a distance is also safer if our partner is liable to outbursts of distressed or violent behaviour.

In spite of the fact that we tend to dismiss sighs or such little noises as the swallowing of saliva as potential for communication, it is rare for people to be making no sound at all. Such sounds as there are tend to get louder once our partner realizes that they will always get a response to their rudimentary self-directed conversation. There comes a point where their attention shifts without effort to the source of 'their sounds or movements' which they recognize and have meaning for them but which are coming from outside.

Words are too clumsy to describe the delicacy of our initial journeys into the inner worlds of our partner. We have already met the words which we associate with our attitude, 'respect', 'openness', 'vulnerability', 'tenderness', 'quietness', 'listening', 'response', but all of these are just tools which we take with us, aids to heightened attention to presence – and a 'present' pulled apart to 'now', so instantaneous that there appears to be no time lag between an occurrence and its perception, since its origin is now common. As we enter this shared pool, we may reach a point where our sense of time is suspended, a dynamic stasis which can only be described in terms of, 'it feels as if'. While the world swirls on round us we find ourselves lost in interpersonal yet private exchange. In describing this affect as resembling that experienced in the bonding relationship between mother and infant in their early engagements, it is a misunderstanding to assume that this is to regard our partner as infantile. In these affective explorations we are in a relationship of total equality. At this point we experience the tender landscape of sensation rather than that of hard-edged cognition, a sensory garden in which perception of shared 'other' overrides awareness of self. Through attention we have arrived at what is known as the dyadic state.

(In naming this state as dyadic, there is the possibility of confusion since in some literature the term is sometimes used as of just two people engaged in conversation. It is the quality of the dialogue that is at issue and the depth of mutual attention leading to exclusion of extraneous intrusions.) In this place it's not just that we 'do' what they 'do' (mimicry) – but that through our responses we enter a mutual sensory world. Since our feeling 'that we are' is derived from the sensory messages we receive, for the time that my self-interest is suspended and our attention jointly focused, there is a sense in which 'I am what they are'. In sharing our sensory experience – and in the 'how' of our response, we share ourselves. This alignment is not only that I feel, hear and see the same as my partner does, but also of affect, an *extra*ordinary experience which is perceived as a reciprocal dance where the intricate movements of one partner set the pattern for the other, turn by turn but always based in regard for other.

This condition, where our perception of timing appears to slow down, is described as 'flow', and by athletes as being 'in the zone' (Buhusi and Meck 2005). Flow can be achieved through many different activities. According to the psychologist Daniel Goleman, the criterion for its achievement is total attention:

> People become utterly absorbed in what they are doing, paying undivided attention to the task, their awareness merged with their actions.... A highly concentrated state is the essence of flow. There seems to be a feedback loop at the gateway to this zone: it can require considerable effort to get calm and focused enough to begin the task – the first step takes some discipline but once focus has started to lock in it takes on a force of its own, both offering relief from emotional turbulence and making the task effortless. (Goleman 1996)

and similarly,

> When people are involved in activities that effortlessly capture and hold their attention, their brain 'quiets down' in the sense that there is a lessening of cortical arousal. (Hamilton *et al*. 1984)

In order to achieve flow, the object of focus is not so important as the degree to which we are able to practise attention – how deeply we are able to focus. However, what is relevant here is a situation where attention is mutual, focused entirely in our partner as our partner's is in us. For different reasons (our partner because their brain is confronted, often for the first time in their kaleidoscope world, by an input that has significance for it; and ourselves because this is our intention, to locate what it is that has meaning for our partner), we have arrived at a place where there is nothing else but the person we are with. There is something about sharing such an experience that lifts it even above that which is felt on its own.

This search for attention is not necessarily a prescription, but rather an attempt to describe what can happen in a successful interaction. If I have laboured the point, it is because I myself am amazed at the effectiveness of such simple intervention. We do not have to go far to witness such transformation. Ron's mother tells me that since his family have been talking to him in a way he can make sense of, he has been able to go back to the school from which he had been excluded – 'His communication is improving all the time and he's really getting to like one or two people.'

The initial shock of hands-on engagement can be astonishing. Time and again, in the face of response, a new practitioner will look up and say, 'It works, it works!' and then fall silent as they consider the implications of their new ability to make contact with hitherto inaccessible partners. As one student said, 'When I first heard about using a person's body language I thought the enthusiasm for its approach was a bit over the top – but I tried it and now I know it works.'

To come back to earth, if I am to hear you, see you, receive your initiatives, I need to be present, present in a way that is not part of our normal everyday exchange. I need to put aside my own reality and listen to you with all my sensory capacity so that I see and hear what actually happens, not as a projection of my own concerns but as a total awareness of any movements or sounds you may make and what these mean to you. If we do this, it is surprising how quickly our ability to make contact improves, especially when our partner responds. Learning to place our focus in our partner becomes habitual. This internal dedication of the senses quickly overrides external distraction, so that it is possible to carry on 'conversations' even in the middle of a crowded classroom.

3

Stress

The tide of stress

It is clear that the people we have met so far are in one way or another experiencing acute stress, not only distressing to them but interfering with their ability to connect with those who share their lives.

Not being able to communicate with other people is in itself stressful, but how can we know what this feels like? Apart from the unpleasant experience of being 'sent to Coventry', what does it feel like to be unable to make ourselves understood by the people round us? And what does it feel like to be able to move from the position of being unable to communicate to that of free interaction?

One might think it was very difficult to reproduce artificially such a situation in a way that was real enough for us to be able to feel what it is like to be in such a state – but recently I attended an in-depth experiential workshop run by psychologist Pete Coia where the participants were given just such an insight (Coia 2006).

The group was divided into pairs who were unknown to each other and placed in lines facing each other, one line facing towards the front and the other with their backs to the board. The impossible task they were given was that the group facing forwards had to convey to their partner the contents of a picture on the board without using speech, eye-contact or recognizable signs. These rules were enforced by rigorous supervisors. After ten minutes the pairs were swapped round, still silent, so that the sender became the recipient for a different picture.

Although we were willing participants in this 'game', it rapidly became real as we struggled to convey information against all the odds. Tension was relieved when we were released to talk to each other about how it had felt. The principal feeling of helplessness was released in laughter (we were volunteers), but then, as we realized how hopeless the situation was, there was a temptation to abandon trying. By the time we were allowed to talk about how we had felt, even though we knew it was just an exercise, there was considerable resentment directed towards the psychologist who had manipulated our affect.

The reaction to being in a hopeless situation had been either to cheat (challenging behaviour that earned a trip to the psychologist – for 'time out' or 'behavioural programmes' – and if this did not work, a visit to the psychiatrist for medication) or withdrawal, giving up the struggle to make our partner understand. When at last we were able to start exchanging our experiences with our partner, there was a surge of complicit warmth which brought us together, united against our trainer.

The switch from what was effectively depression and avoidance of others to relief at being able to express our feelings at the end was palpable. Although we were unknown to each other, strangers were instantly transformed into complicit and intimate friends. No longer were we alone; we had an ally, someone on our side. I shall remember my partner with whom I shared a stressful situation: it was 'us' against our 'tormentor' and the world outside.

In fact, the experience of stress is common to all of us, with or without disability. It is one of the conditions of being human and is essentially part of a self-correcting mechanism which tells us when we perceive events going wrong for us and urges us to take steps to remedy the situation. But it is also the tide on which our behaviour sails. If our stress levels are low we are likely to remain calm when our brains tell us a threatening event is occurring or is about to occur. If something bad happens to us when we are highly stressed, we easily slip into an aggressive response.

So how does it affect our stress levels if our sensory intake is faulty (as in visual or auditory disability, for example), or if for one reason or another input is correctly received but incorrectly interpreted because, as Lindsay Weekes once put it (Weekes, date unknown), our brains are 'not wired up properly'? Since we are by nature self-protecting, if we have problems interpreting our surroundings, every event is potentially dangerous.

Stress and the body's defences

It is well known that when our brain perceives our body to be in danger, it prepares the body to react in such a way as to deal with what it sees as emergency. The body is flooded by the hormone adrenalin, which raises the heart-beat and generally speeds up the circulation of blood. Extra oxygen is carried to all parts of the body so that we can respond immediately by running away or taking aggressive action. This is known as the fight/flight response or defence response and is essential for our survival. At the same time there is a slower response that releases another hormone, cortisol, which in its turn releases energy producing glucose to fund any necessary activity.

Because there are now a number of extremely self-reflective and articulate accounts of what it is like to be on the autistic spectrum, in some ways it is more difficult for us to penetrate what it is like to have very severe learning disabilities than to have severe autism. Accounts by people who have mild disability are mainly factual accounts of the humiliations they experience rather than how this actually impacts on how they feel. But Bennett (1998) points out that simply to experience severe learning disabilities is extremely likely to be accompanied by severe stress. She cites the very simple example of thirst. Inability to communicate need or understand explanations can lead to physical distress. Frustration leads to psychological distress. Apart from acute episodes, there is likely to be a long-term build-up of chronic stress from childhood on.

One of the difficulties in our understanding of behaviour we call challenging is that we all have different thresholds for what the brain sees as stressful and threatening enough to trigger the fight/flight system, so it is difficult for me to make the necessary leap of imagination to understand why you are so scared. What situations are there that I see as so frightening that I need to take instant remedial action to get out of it – but you are unmoved by? Some we would agree on – both of us would probably jump out of the way of an advancing car that threatened to run us over. But sitting in an aeroplane on a runway when the engines start revving for take-off, I experience all the symptoms of stress, dry mouth, pounding heart, and so on. If I could stop the plane and get off, I should. Whereas you may look out of the window and admire the view as the plane rises over the city. We have different thresholds for triggering our defence system. One person's stress is another's opportunity.

To pursue this a little – I find it impossible to understand that the same set of circumstances that cause me to sweat with fear offer enjoyment to you. Because my blueprints are so deeply embedded, I cannot put myself in your place, see the world from your point of view. It

is this mismatch of understanding that is at the root of so much of our difficulty in empathizing and therefore helping those who have a different
mental picture of the world. We may mean to help them, but we do so
within the framework of our own reality, not theirs. Even if we are
conscious of this, which mostly we are not, we make our judgements and
base our strategies on our own familiar economy. So we don't understand
how it is that, for example, if touched lightly a person with autism may
feel they are drowning in a tidal wave of painful response and a total loss
of control as their understanding is swept away. It is simply beyond our
experience, beyond even what we can imagine. When he is becoming
upset, a small boy tells his mother that his ears are 'fizzy'. Another shouts
at his mother, 'My head's running away, my head's running away!', a
life-threatening sensation for him that leaves his mother baffled. She says,
'What does he mean?' when he is clearly trying to tell us of the physical
sensation he is experiencing as his brain collapses into fragmentation.
This is how it feels for him.

Events that we may see as normal or not even notice may be perceived
as acutely stressful and the prelude to outbursts of violent and distressed
behaviour. The brain tells the body that it is in mortal danger and the
body responds as if this were so, by attacking or running away. This
problem is particularly acute in some people on the autistic spectrum
whose defence system is on a knife-edge since they feel themselves to be
so endangered. Ros Blackburn, a well known speaker with autism,
speaking at a Kindered Spirits Workshop in Tytheringron in 2006, said:
'To me the outside world is a totally baffling incomprehensible mayhem
which terrifies me. It is a meaningless mess of sights, sounds, noises and
movements, coming from nowhere going nowhere'. In a 2006 television
documentary on BBC2 Temple Grandin said that the predominant
emotion in autism is fear. She is always looking for something terrifying.
Therese Jolliffe says she lives in terror all the time.

So if our brains have learned that something terrifying may happen,
we may live in fear, not just of the event when it happens but also that it
may happen. In this case the perceived stress will be chronic, so that the
body is exposed to ongoing raised levels of cortisol. This happens particularly if people feel they lack control to make decisions, one of the key
features of severe learning disability. High levels of chronic stress are particularly damaging during childhood, and apart from setting up blueprints of continuing fear, this is a situation that can have long-term health

effects, damaging the immune system, raising blood pressure and affecting the memory. This omnipresent low-level threat can make it much harder to recover from acute stress.

Coping strategies

In an effort to lower the stress level and reassert control, we need to look at the various coping strategies open to a non-verbal person.

First of all, our partner may try to focus on a repetitive behaviour. This will enable them to withdraw attention from the world outside, retreating into an inner world. Here they can focus either on a sensation drawn directly from the brain–body language, on something as simple as their own breathing rhythm or the feedback sensation derived from scratching their hands. One of the more bizarre possibilities is that the body adopts an attitude, a physical stance that (by pressure) achieves a point of focus to which the individual can pay attention rather than to the sensory chaos that troubles them.

Both Gunilla Gerland and Donna Williams describe the onset of fragmentation as a fizzy feeling like lemonade in the back of the neck which develops into a pain that spreads throughout the body. Les is an eleven-year-old boy who walks with a curious posture, his head tilted backwards and downwards. If one tries this out oneself, one realizes this position exerts pressure on the nape of the neck. Like the children who hit the back of their necks before an outburst, it seems reasonable to assume that Les is giving himself a physical sensation in an effort to prevent his sensory experience breaking up. His body has learned a way to try and control the process of going into fragmentation.

Alternatively, in an effort to maintain coherence, sensation can be derived from an object or activity in the world outside. In the latter case we need to interpret this, not as a direct interest in the outside world, rather as a sensation drawn in, hijacked from the outer world and used to feed the interior world, protecting it from over-stimulation by input for which it does not have the interpretative capacity. A good example of this is to be found in the 1992 Channel 4 film *A is for Autism*, in which Temple Grandin is heard talking about how she endlessly spun a coin when she was a child. She tells us that by visually focusing on the movement and by listening to the sound, she was able to cut out other sounds, even noisy percussive ones. Lindsay Weekes says that at a disco, he would always focus on the lights, which enabled him to ignore the sound and noise going on round him.

Another strategy for individuals who are themselves over-stimulated is to withdraw themselves from what is perceived as the source of over-stimulus by physically removing themselves in one way or another. For example, they may shut their eyes, turn away, pull a shirt over their heads or run away and hide in a quiet place. A common complaint is 'He spends all his time in his room' – when if we think about it, his body language is telling us that he is overloaded, maybe by the cheerful but noisy colour and patterns of the furnishings in the sitting room.

Finally, and often in desperation, the person may become physically aggressive. In an effort to reduce overload the person physically attacks whatever is perceived to be the source of the stimulus, or someone who seen as preventing him or her from reaching a quiet sanctuary where he or she can de-stress. In a variation of this the person attacks himself or herself in order to reduce the distress by overriding the painful feedback to which he or she is particularly sensitive and returning the world to coherence.

In situations that their brains perceive as stressful, the exact coping strategies that individuals use to de-stress themselves are a matter of temperament, coupled with the route they have learned is most effective in obtaining release. Many will start with a repetitive behaviour, which gradually becomes wilder as their stress level builds, go on to an avoidance tactic, and if all else fails use aggression as a last resort. Others will retreat at an early stage, and yet others will show little build-up but launch into a full-scale attack apparently without warning (although very careful observation sometimes reveals early warning signals which are small enough to have been overlooked).

Stress and stress reactions are particularly a feature of life on the autistic spectrum, where there is a constant battle going on in the brain which, in the teeth of contradicting evidence supplied through a faulty processing system, is trying to make sense of its environment. Therese Jolliffe talks of spending her whole life, all her time, 'trying to make sense of what is going on'.

There are some people who feel so desperately threatened when they lose track of what is happening, that they will lash out even if (to our eyes) for the 'trivial reason' that the person to whom they have been talking turns away without letting them know that they are going to do so. What we have to understand is that for our partner this withdrawal represents a cataclysmic loss of control, which their brain has told them is life-threatening. Once we understand this, we can make sure that we tell them exactly what we are about to do, and if possible get their assent, at least making sure that they understand before we do it. Comprehension may be just a flick of the eyelids – but, for these people, as soon as they know we will not do something unexpected which tips the brain into chaos, that we know the 'rules of their game', their stress level drops and they become more confident. The frequency of distressed outbreaks falls, even to the point of non-occurrence.

And yet still we are trying to control behaviour rather than look for its causes.

Identifying causes of stress

When we are working with people whose stress level is so great that the only way they know how to deal with it is to attack what they perceive to be the source of their distress (or self-harm in order to neutralize their overwhelming sensations), we tend to focus on prevention and restraint. Such strategies as we can come up with, if they do not address underlying causes, may temporarily prevent the behaviour, but the distress will almost always manifest itself in a different way.

It is absolutely essential when we work with people who are having distressed outbursts that we not only work out what we should do at the time a person is upset, but also identify the underlying causes leading to their distress. I need to know not only what to do if this person is upset or violent but also what the trigger for their aggression may be.

Stan bites himself. He is hypersensitive to certain frequencies. Every time he hears them he screams and digs his teeth into his flesh. He has a callus the size of half a tennis ball on his wrist which bleeds. It is not enough just to restrain him from this behaviour, since this does not address his vulnerability and leaves him exposed to events which he experiences as extremely painful. To help him it is imperative that we explore the particular triggers for his distress and reduce their incidence by separating him from the source. To leave him in a situation that is exposing him to pain is a form of abuse.

Recognizing the desperate attempts made by the body itself to regain control over its warring systems, we need to turn our attention to a discussion of the strategies we can employ to assist those people whose confusion, frustration or pain is triggering such stress that their only resort is to what we call 'challenging behaviour'.

If we draw up a balance sheet, on the negative side we have a highly stressed psyche on the run from information it is interpreting as hostile, burying itself in its inner world and lashing out at perceived threat. On the positive side, if we can reduce the stress that the individual is experiencing, we are often able to introduce them to a world outside which is perceived as user-friendly. We can do this in two ways. The first involves modifying the environment so that the person is not subject to events which can be causing them pain. However this is achieved, reduction in the incidence of particular sounds (as those which were upsetting Stan) can lead to a marked drop in distressed behaviour. A number of people I have worked with can process incoming information more easily in certain coloured light, so putting in a different bulb (quite often, but not always, green) can reduce aggression. The second approach is to introduce a communication system based on the partner's body language, directing attention away from the painful triggers to significant landmarks of a recognizable terrain, through the approach know as Intensive Interaction. Given the pain and confusion triggered by a hypersensitivity, one of the remarkable aspects of such a shift is that relocating the attention from the inside world to that outside really can be so powerful as to override it. For example, Pranve, who appears in *Finding You Finding Me*, is hypersensitive to sound. Every time an aeroplane passes low over the house as it comes in to land at the airport, his eyes roll up to the left, particularly if the engine has a high whine. Yet twenty minutes into a conversation using his sounds and hand movements he is so focused on what we are doing that he is unmoved by the noise any more. His eyes do not flicker even when the plane is right overhead.

Both these options are open to us. What we should not do, is do nothing.

4

Body Language

Feelings

When we speak to each other, we express what we need and what we feel – and we listen and respond to the needs and feelings of our partner. We do this not only through words but also, even if we are not consciously noticing it, through gesture, facial language and body posture. The expression 'She was able to read her like a book' pays homage to our capacity to interpret body language. Some people are easier to read than others, we call them transparent – their feelings are clearly expressed through body and facial language. At the other end of the scale we might say of someone that they are inscrutable, they hide their feelings well. This works both ways: we are so used to receiving body response as well as verbal language to our communications, that if our conversation partner blanks themselves off, it immediately arouses suspicion and sets the alarm bells ringing – 'What has he got to hide?' I think this already points to a feature of body language, which is that it is an expression of affect, it tells people how we feel. So where does it all start?

The infant–mother paradigm

We feel cut off from people if they are non-verbal. But if we look at a mother and baby it is apparent that, all being well, they are totally in touch with each other from the moment of birth. In the field of child development, much study has gone into this imitative non-verbal conversation which arises at the earliest possible stage.

At birth we leave the nourishment of our mother's womb and enter a startling sensory world. Learning begins at once. We blink, protest, cry when we are uncomfortable, gurgle with pleasure – and our mother responds and we answer – embarking almost immediately on the long journey of communication. Part of this evolution appears to be an inbuilt curiosity and fascination with imitation. Even as early as twenty minutes after the traumatic passage out of the birth canal, we will stick out our tongue if our mother sticks out hers.

Starting from such simple gestures, the capacity to imitate evolves into an intimate conversation, through which both of us explore and convey our feelings to each other. It is the gateway to our relationship and future relationships.

Using our body language, we become totally involved in what is known as a dyadic relationship, a partnership which is focused on the discovery of ourselves and others to the exclusion of observers, in what the psychologist Suzanne Zeedyk (2006) has graphically described as 'the glass bubble'. Using imitation of sound and touch and gesture we enter a creative and intimate playground in which we share ourselves, discover play and laughter and lay the foundation and rules for all future communication. Contained in the safety net of the dyad, we learn about the world, building hypotheses, trying things out and testing our boundaries, referring back to see what effect our activities have. 'What will happen if I do this?', monitoring our mother's face for answers.

So why is it that imitation is so powerful that it immediately grabs our attention? Why do I immediately recognize if you do what I do or something which is part of my repertoire? Why do you find it so riveting if I echo your behaviour, that it penetrates through the fog of sensory chaos and captures your attention at once, quite often even if you are disturbed at the time?

What's in a name?

First of all we need a name for communication approaches which use as a basis what psychologists rather loosely call imitation and, following from this, the use of body language to get in touch with our partners. Such approaches seem to have arisen about the same time in different places. In the UK the use of imitation and body language was introduced almost accidentally by Geraint Ephraim, a psychologist working with people with severe disability and distressed behaviour. A somewhat symbolic photograph shows him pausing on a walk through the Llanberis slate mines, leaning over some rusting iron scaffolding and peering across a deep dark mine-shaft into the middle distance (see Frontispiece). One day at Harpebury Hospital, frustrated at being unable to reach a young man with autism, he started to echo back his behaviour and was very surprised when his partner sat up and started to take notice (Ephraim 1986). He tried this approach successfully with other residents and after some thought decided to call it 'Augmented Mothering', a choice that reflected its origins in the mother–infant relationship. Unfortunately the timing was bad, coinciding as it did with intense interest in 'Normalization' and 'Age Appropriateness'. Since his initial work was with adults, providers at the time felt that such an approach must be age-inappropriate and this led to its being sidelined. Nind and Hewett (1994) proposed the current name, 'Intensive Interaction'.

I have already mentioned 'Co-creative Communication' used in Scandinavia (Nafstad and Rødbroe 1999). In America, the Son-Rise technique has related features in that it uses imitation as the basis of its approach. One of the key features of this approach is the use of a dedicated room so that interaction can take place away from all outside distractions. However, practitioners of Intensive Interaction do not find this necessary, since the people they approach, their partners, are so attracted when they hear/see/feel part of their own repertoire that they latch on to such intervention almost immediately. This interest is almost always accompanied by positive behavioural change. For example, I was asked to see three children in a class, whose first language was Urdu. All were on the autistic spectrum and severely disruptive. In the morning I taught their class support teachers how to work with them by using their sounds and movements. At the end of the day their teacher observed that she had never seen them sitting quietly before. It should also be pointed out that the way that it is set up, Son-Rise interventions involve considerable expense, whereas such positive outcomes as those achieved using Intensive Interaction are, apart from an initial training day (often run through parents groups or professional groups), without cost.

Much closer to Intensive Interaction is the approach known as 'Proximal Communication' (Potter and Whittaker 2001). In a list of differences, Potter and Whittaker suggest that Intensive Interaction advocates the use of a 'running commentary', where the skilled partner uses 'our language' to highlight the interactive process. In practice it has proved quite difficult to define exactly what is involved in using Intensive Interaction. The current boundaries of what is currently practised are somewhat fluid, and some practitioners use approaches which do not necessarily conform to the model illustrated by Potter and Whittaker. One of the problems here is that Ephraim, who introduced the approach, was rather vague and left very little in the way of supporting literature, so that those who learned directly from him and from his work, have tended to develop individual styles. Personally, I hardly ever use speech while communicating and, as the authors of Proximal Communication put it, transmission of empathy is through non-verbal communication. Once interaction is established I sometimes use our language and my partner's bilingually, mixed up together rather like Welsh and English are used in parts of Wales. So for example, I may gift-wrap an idea in our language they find stressful, such as 'bath', within the package of their language as in 'Er-er, Martin Bath, Er-er'.

Potter and Whittaker raise the question of research. Dundee Psychology Department is currently evaluating the videos of interaction on a frame-by-frame analysis as a preliminary study to a long-term evaluation. This will involve a time-line study of work in a day centre with a group of both autistic and non-autistic children. Preliminary findings suggest that while the speed at which improvement in sociability occurs varies, the pattern is always the same: that the consequence of using imitation is accompanied by an increase in sociability in both adults and children.

Even where we have a name there is considerable variation in the exact way that those who practise Intensive Interaction are going about it. For example, in a recent evaluation of the effectiveness of this approach in the *British Journal of Learning Disabilities*, the authors used a box 'containing a variety of sensory items, balls silk materials, musical chimes' to promote activity, that is they introduced a third party to what is intended to be one-on-one interaction based on personal behaviour or, if they are used, objects that are already part of our partner's repertoire (Leaning and Watson 2006).

Repetitive behaviours

The majority of people who are non-verbal and have withdrawn into an inner world will be giving attention to some form of stimulus, listening to their brain–body communications or focusing on stimuli that they have borrowed from the world outside and are using to self-stimulate. Opinion has been divided as to whether to join in or to try and divert attention from them. However, eliminating such behaviours leaves our partners vulnerable to their hypersensitivities (Gillingham 1995). I use what might be seen as a third option, which is to regard them as part of our partner's language and to use them creatively. This may be seen as diversion. Perhaps the main emphasis in the way I practise and teach is that I encourage students to immerse themselves in their partner's body and facial language. Just like verbal language, they will find it has different elements expressed in different ways, a vocabulary and grammar of its own. What is important is what it is that is familiar and recognizable to our partner's brain. They may grunt and scratch their hand. If they grunt, we might either answer them with a similar grunt or we might answer their grunt by a contingent touch on the hand. We do not necessarily always use the same element of their language to respond to their initiative, but they will always get an answer, based on an element borrowed from their language, even if it is not the same one as they used. This means that they learn extremely quickly that when they make some movement or sound, they get a response that is significant and meaningful for their brain. Quite often they will understand the connection and refer back virtually immediately they get a significant response. In the chaos of my sensory experience, here is something significant. I want it.

At present those of us who use body language to communicate find ourselves in the strange position of daily being presented with an approach which is changing lives but is still out on a very long limb as far as theoreticians are concerned. From our point of view they have a lot of catching up to do – but research takes time, and when one is presented with vulnerable young people whose distressed and difficult to manage behaviour is ruining their lives, it is difficult to justify delay. And when a child is referred by Education Services or Health or Social Services because of their behavioural distress, how would I choose which child to use as an untreated control? And if the people who support them ring back a fortnight later and say this child has already stopped hitting himself, is this not evidence? In her keynote address to the Leeds Conference on Intensive Interaction in 2006, educational psychologist Melanie Nind suggested that we had got beyond the stage where we were continually needing to prove how well it worked. I agree with this statement, but unfortunately there are still many providers outside the educational field who have not yet heard of Intensive Interaction. In order to spread the advantages of using this approach to everyone who is working in the field of non-verbal communication we still need more research, even if it is running a long way behind practice. We need to make it commonplace.

Using body language as a conversation

I want to look in more detail now at how we build body language into conversation. In Chapter 1 we saw how Ron responded to his sounds instantly, and how Nick calmed down when he discovered that he could get a response to his sounds and from this he generalized from an auditory conversation to a visual mode (he wriggled his foot and looked to see if we would wriggle ours).

But it wasn't just imitation, I did not always answer in quite the same way. If he moved his foot up, I might move mine sideways or jerk it a little, just enough for him to see the response in the same mode but with a small spicing up of difference. Later I might swap modes so that his movement was 'answered' by my tapping his chair – a sound for a movement. These small differences within the context of a known language harden attention to engagement and prevent the brain becoming habituated. It quickly became clear that Nick understood and welcomed the principle involved – 'if I originate a sound or movement I will get a response'. This is the missing link, the absence of which is responsible both for our failure to make contact with our partners and for their failure to make connection with us.

('Up until now all my pre-verbal attempts to get in touch with you have been dismissed, so I have been using them to talk to myself. Now the bridge has been established I can talk to you.')

So when we use body language to communicate, we are trying to relocate our partner's focus of attention from the inner world to which he or she has retreated, to the world outside. But as mentioned above, the parameters of such an approach are not always very well defined, a situation that causes some confusion among less experienced practitioners. Some feel that all they have to do is mimic – but are soon asking what they should do next.

Even with the same partner, because our conversations are intensely personal, each practitioner is probably communicating slightly differently, just as when we speak to different people. For myself, I think of it as using what is a rather loose 'imitation' within the context of a conversation based on the particular language that has meaning for my partner. So it includes all their body language and responses – but in a more subtle sense it also includes their logic – basing their interpretations (as far as it is physically possible to deduce them) on their sensory experience of the world rather than mine.

To make sense of it, I need to know the *why* of their language. For example, Matty kicks the wall to know where it is, because he does not see the boundary between the wall and floor as a straight line but one that wriggles around. His behaviour, which it was suggested was naughtiness, is completely logical within the parameters of his sensory experience. I can see what Matty is doing but I also need to work out why. It is like reading words without understanding their meaning, so we interpret the action in the light of the significance it has for us. Now that I know why he is kicking the wall, I can pay attention to how he is doing it. Does it make a difference if he is calm or agitated? Understanding what is going on enables us to align ourselves with the our partner's affective state so that we can use empathy to put ourselves alongside our partner.

From our partner's point of view (if they are autistic), in order to cut down on the sensory input and avoid becoming overloaded (to 'maintain coherence' as Lindsay Weekes puts it), there is a very wide range of actions on which the brain can home in: almost any activity which is capable of repetition, or elements of body language which are not repetitive. They may be pre-linguistic sounds or even just an action expressive of feeling, such as a sigh. It can be a secret internal rhythm which most of us take for granted, such as breathing. At the other end of the scale it can be an activity or behaviour (or in the case of a more able person, an occupation or theme) hijacked from the world outside and used to feed the internal world.

Lizzie sticks her finger into a minute hole in the wall. She is searching for little bits to place on her tongue. When she has them in place she feels them against the roof of her mouth. It is a sensation that helps her to focus, so that in the middle of sensory chaos there is at least one sensation that enables her to know what she is doing. She never swallows them even when she is eating. We cannot get Lizzie's attention until her partner lies on the floor beside her and sticks her finger into the hole. Immediately Lizzie smiles and her whole body language changes from exclusion to interaction.

Whatever the point of focus, this is where the individual's attention is directed, this is what they are 'listening to'. It may be a sound or a movement, rearranging chairs or tearing paper that is part of their repertoire – but whatever it is, it is claiming their interest and keeps over-loading stimuli from the outside world at bay.

Whatever it is that is claiming our partner's attention, from the point of view of the practitioner partner the underlying and critical question is: how can we reach into the inner world of this person so that we can claim their attention? We must remember that the nature of the activity is irrele-vant: what we are about is developing relationship rather than confor-mity. In order to encourage this we are not so much interested in what they are doing but in how they are feeling.

Observation

Recent research (Falck-Ytter *et al.* 2006) indicates a behaviour pattern which, when we reflect on it seems obvious to us: that we recognize an activity done by others if it is already part of our own repertoire. The researchers compared the ability of six-month-old babies to recognize intention with those a year old.

At six months a baby will track a toy being picked up and placed in a bucket. But by twelve months, when the toy is picked up, the baby's eyes leap ahead to the bucket. This happens only if the toys are being handled and not if they are thrown or moved independently of the hand. The one-year-olds know what will happen. The authors suggest that this anticipatory capacity is a function of the infant's mirror neurones, nerves in the head that fire both when an action is performed and when the infant sees the same action performed by someone else. Critically, the year-olds have already mastered the skill of placing toys in a bucket but the younger ones will not have done so yet. 'This allows them to map their observation of someone else performing the action into their own neural representation for performing the action' (Falck-Ytter *et al.* 2006). So anticipation requires that we already have a template, a neural map from which to project the trajectory of an event.

Commenting on this, Pete Coia spells out the implication that, hardly surprisingly, meaningfulness depends on previous experience:

> It is not surprising that using a person's body language to talk to them, must capture something one's partner can already experi-ence and is familiar to them – and that this experience can be wid-ened and deepened by variation and extension over time,

>provided the extension is related to the original and the variation
>is not too great. (Personal communication)

What is particularly interesting about these investigations is that the recognized behaviour was not necessarily contingent to the time it was originally learned. It can be something learned previously and stored as a template. In my training video, *Learning the Language*, working with Gabriel I blew in his right ear when his head was turned sideways. I did this because previously I had seen him take a balloon, half inflate it and let the air out into his ear – so I knew that it was a stimulus he would recognize even though it was not part of our current conversation. When I did this he turned his head and placed his left ear close to my mouth so that I would repeat the stimulus in that side.

If I want to get in touch with you, I am going to have to tap into some element of your experience already mapped into your brain, so-called 'hard-wired' in. I have to find out how it is that you are talking to yourself and use the language of your internal dialogue, such as a rhythm, movement or sound, to build a bridge, so you can talk to me and I can talk to you. To do this I have to observe in the most minute detail what you are doing as expressed in your body language. I must look not only at your repetitive behaviours but also at anything in which you are showing interest, because this is an action or initiative you will recognize. Where is your attention focused?

So I start by asking myself what my partner is doing (the action), how is she doing it (which tells me how she feels) and, perhaps not quite so obviously, exactly where is the focus of my partner's self-stimulation?

What is my partner is doing?

What they are focusing on is quite often fairly simple, provided that we are prepared to suspend our own judgement of what is or is not significant. The slightest sound of sucking saliva, or the explosive exhalation after breath holding may be what is meaningful for that individual. It may not have any interest for us, but this does not mean it is not a landmark for them. If we miss this, we miss our chance of getting into conversation with them.

The possibilities are endless. A child with autism presses his nose against the floor. Bending the cartilage gives him a sensation of severe pressure which, in a chaotic world, tells him what he is doing. It is a sensation that his brain can process, it makes sense to him. In focusing on the pain he is engendering he does not have to take on board the sensory chaos which invades him. Another child runs his finger around cut-out circles in plastic foam. A woman with multiple disabilities listens to her sighs. A boy focuses on the rotational movement of dialling a toy telephone and smiles with pleasure when I rotate my finger in the air. His brain recognizes that the pattern of my movement is related to the physical sensation he derives from his movement, and is particularly entranced when I reverse the direction of rotation. This is seriously funny and we share the visual joke. Sharing humour is a fundamental way people make friends. The sharing does not have to be verbal. Another man runs his tongue round his lips and laughs at a similar reversal of direction on my part. Similarly, a child blowing a toy windmill recognizes when I rotate my finger and laughs at the change of direction. In each case, the brain recognizes a familiar pattern but is intrigued by change (within the parameters of expectation). The joke is recognizable provided it stays within the user-friendly repertoire of their personal language.

One of the most common conversations between brain and body consists of rubbing the fingers and thumbs together. The brain says 'rub' and the skin sends feedback to the brain saying that the fingers have 'done it'. These are all physical sensations; but a more able individual may focus on some external activity such as a particular video. A boy in the video *A is for Autism* is totally absorbed in drawing trains and track. Interestingly, even when his drawing comes to a level crossing and temporarily diverts to a road, he says it goes to nowhere and quickly reverts to railway track. For him, the track with its laid-down rails is more well-defined and less random than a road with all its possibilities.

We may have to work though a number of different behavioural elements before we come to the one that they are able to use for communication rather than defence. Out of this multiplicity of feedbacks which can be regarded as potential material for interaction, it is not so much the particular activity on which they focus attention which is important, rather its internal function. Whichever one it is, if it is the centre of our partner's focus, they do not have to see/hear all the things they find confusing, threatening or painful. They can simply switch into a world which, unlike our shared reality, is comprehensible for them. Some people see this as trying to control the world, but I think the word 'control' is misleading since it drags an undercurrent of manipulation, whereas this total concentration is better viewed as a last-ditch attempt to maintain coherence in the middle of sensory chaos.

Many people will have not just one point of convergence but a number. A boy is totally absorbed in watching a particular cartoon, which he does to the exclusion of interest in what is going on round him. (His fixation on the film enables him to be able to exclude overloading external and internal sensations.) But he will also blow raspberry sounds on his arm, 'talking to himself'. Both his fixation and his auto-communication are points of attention; but whereas it is impossible to share his dedication to the film, the latter can be a way of access to his inner world. When I make a similar noise on my arm, his interest is captured, and in spite of the TV still being on, he leaves it to come and explore the source of 'his' sound. An alternative strategy is for the person to hang on to a point of reference from the outside world such as a special comforter to refocus attention, an object to be manipulated, such as a ball of string, or touching a lampstand when anxious. All of these landmarks serve a similar end, to reduce the sensory overload the person is experiencing.

('When I do this, whatever it is, I know what I am doing. I can focus on this strategy to the exclusion of my sensory turmoil.')

Because repetitive behaviours act as barriers to communication, many support staff still feel that they should try to reduce or eliminate them. It is really vital that we understand that to do so leaves the person vulnerable to the severe sensory pains associated with hypersensitivities. It is like removing a filling, leaving the nerve bare and then expecting our partners to enjoy a nice hot cup of tea. The safe way to approach the problem is to see them as part of a language and to use repetitive behaviours creatively (Gillingham 1995).

How is my partner doing their activity?

At the beginning of this book I raised the issue of it being very easy to hear the words a person is 'saying' rather than listening to how they feel. This also applies to non-verbal conversations if we respond to what they do but ignore how they are doing it, if we mirror form rather than meaning.

As mentioned above, a person's body language not only tells us how they are talking to themselves but also gives us an insight into their emotional state. It lets us know how they feel: it is not just 'what' a person is doing but how it is done that is the giveaway. For example flapping the hand varies from a gentle twitch to an agitated swing, the movement and accompanying sounds increasing in concert with the degree of disturbance being experienced. In fact, this element of communication should be nothing new to us. We are all constantly monitoring the body language of the people we talk to, since it tells us not just what they are saying but also how they feel. For example, I may lift my eyebrows and open my eyes wider in surprise and wonder – an action which according to Goleman (1996) allows more light in so that my brain receives more visual information about an unknown situation and can therefore assess its potential for threat more easily) – or I may lift them in disdain, a similar action but one which in this case is accompanied by a slight backward movement of the neck, tightening of the lips and cold eyes. No words need to be said, but we do not confuse the two because when we talk to people we are reading how people feel all the time through their facial and postural language. In Chapter 6 we shall look at whether or not people (with autism especially) can read the body language of others and what are the limits to this. For the present, each person is special. Their 'language' has its own inflections, rhythms and style. As we get to know each other better, we begin to address the subtleties of an individual's particular language: how it is performed and put together is unique to that person and also characteristic of how they are currently feeling.

Where is my partner self-stimulating?

The physical site of a person's internal conversation with themselves may be critical because, as I have explained previously (Caldwell 2002a, 2002b), this may be where they feel themselves to be. Briefly, the reason for this is that we know *that* we are as an outcome of the feedback we receive from the world outside. I know that I am because, sitting on this chair I feel the seat on my backside and my feet on the floor. This message not only tells me about the world outside but also informs me that particular organs are receiving the message. It tells me about myself through proprioceptive and balance organs, as well as the material world. (A simpler example is that if I see a cup, it tells me about the cup but also that my eyes are seeing the cup.) However, because of faulty processing, the messages some people receive from their external feedback may be so confusing that the only sensations they can rely on are those of their internal world, which are, so to speak, 'hard-wired in'. This can be so to the extent that their sense of self may be projected into the site of their self-stimulus. If a person is fixated on their foot or shoulder, this may be the only place through which we can communicate with them, because this is the hub of where they feel themselves to be.

Although it may sound complicated, in actual practice reading people's body language is not difficult since it is a very natural way of getting in touch with each other. We may have to put aside inhibitions about what we 'ought' to be doing and also (which is perhaps more difficult for those who feel they should be 'teaching') reject any attempt to impose an agenda. We are not actually trying to do anything apart from getting alongside a person, learning to read the contours, features and fault-lines of the intuitive map with which our partner presents us. We learn to know what stresses a person and where they feel comfortable. We find out how to be with them in a way that is comfortable for both of us.

Unusually, I take very little in the way of 'case history' before starting interaction, except perhaps finding out if there is some particular thing which will upset the person I am working with. For example, making the video *Learning the Language*, when I met Gabriel for the first time I knew only his name, that he was on the autistic spectrum and that he had severe epilepsy.

While approaching a new partner without a detailed case history can be scary, there is a reason for it. If one approaches a person with an agenda already in place it colours what one perceives and may prevent one noticing exactly what it is that one's partner is doing. Because I am looking for indications as to how my partner feels as well as what they are doing, all this needs to relate to the present and not to some activity they were doing or felt at some other time. My attitude is one of openness to whatever my partner will bring. I 'listen and look' very carefully, giving my partner my total attention to see what they are doing now. I think of our interaction as language which enables us to hold a conversation.

So, in Chapter 1, the description of the intervention with Ron is that of a first-time encounter, as are the others in this book except where stated. The meeting with Nick and his support partner is tentative at first. We show him we value his negative feelings, accepting them as an indication that we should reduce the stress we are placing on him through our proximity. By moving out of his sight but remaining within earshot, we send him a signal that we respect how he feels – but at the same time we do not lose touch. I tell him – and demonstrate with a gesture – that we will be outside in the passage, and once there we continue to keep in touch by using his sounds. Within ten minutes he has joined us and we are growing in mutual trust and burgeoning confidence.

Learning to use our own body language

It is clear that if we are going to talk to people we need not only to be able to read their body language but also to use our own creatively. Turning back to our own verbal conversations, sometimes we come across people whose responses always seem to kill a conversation dead – after they have spoken there just is nowhere to go. We turn away feeling to some extent cheated of what could have been fruitful interchange. In the same way, while starting with imitation, we need to learn to keep our non-verbal interactions open-ended so that they invite a reply, offering the possibility of further exchange.

In the matter of practice we have a great deal to learn from those who support children who are blind and deaf-blind. Of necessity here, sharing information and affect will be tactile. In a fascinating paper, Barbara Miles (1999) explores this approach, partly through the work of Selma Fraiberg (1977). Since they are unable to see, any sense that objects exist as separate entities apart from self – and therefore developing a sense of self – has to be through touch. Fraiberg developed an understanding of the extent to which the hands of a blind or deaf-blind child take over the function of facial language and can express through the use of pressure and tempo all the properties of seeing, smiling, eye gaze, interest, as well as seeking, wooing, preference and recognition. It is absolutely vital to the well-being of the child that parents and support workers learn to read this in order to promote bonding. Barbara Miles takes this up: 'We have to practice noticing the hands – it does not come naturally as we are used to reading faces. And we have to use ours – they are our voice'.

Rather than hand-on-hand touch, which can be directive, a better position is hands-under-hands, where the support partner holds their hands palm up, so that the tips of the fingers of the child's hand rest gently on theirs. This lets the child know they are sharing an experience – it is something both partners are doing together. The attitude is of offering – here are my hands – use them how you like. Explore what they can do.

In order to promote hand development and expressiveness, Barbara Miles (1999) recommends using 'imitation':

> Imitation is the best form of encouragement. It serves to bring the child's awareness to his or her own hands and reinforces for her their power as avenues of expression. Games such as clapping, opening and closing of fingers, crawling with fingers and tickling may follow from imitation of a child's own movements.

And yet even here, the word 'imitation' is being used very loosely, since she goes on to describe how we vary the way we make our response in order to empathize.

What is so important about this work with people who are deaf-blind is that it strips away so many of the superficial questions about technique. Working with people whose only communication is through touch narrows the number of variables and places us firmly into a partnership where total attention is directed to the dyadic experience. Above all, Barbara Miles stresses, each time we touch we communicate something *through the 'way' we touch*. It can be happiness, anger, sadness, impatience, disappointment or maybe it is just a gesture, such as one might nod one's head to say 'I see what you mean' to keep in touch and let our partner know we are there for them.

However we have learned a language, there may be circumstances when we want to use it to turn the conversation so that it goes down a completely different path. So we will use our body language to do this, although preferably as an extension of our partner's gestures as in the following incident.

This concerns a young man, Don, who is on the autistic spectrum. He is very withdrawn but communicates sometimes by tapping people. As he becomes more aroused, his tapping unfortunately grows in strength to slapping and to the point at which he is hurting others. When he starts doing this to me, I use his rhythm to tap back very softly, but I gradually extend the tap into a stroke up his arm. He is getting a significant reply to his initiatives, which, although it is initially one he expects, grows into something else, anchored at first in his tap gesture but sufficiently different to be surprising and therefore attract attention. This has the effect of slowing him down while he thinks about it and subsequently becomes an effective way for his support partners to calm him.

We need to learn not only to read the body language of others but also to use our own to speak to our partners. For example, in the film *Creative Conversations* (Caldwell and Stevens 2005), a young man gazes at his support partner; but, being a newcomer to this approach, she does not find it easy to hold such a prolonged deep gaze. It is apparent that she feels uncomfortable with it. I show her how she can use a gentle downward sweeping hand gesture at the same time as turning slightly away to indicate (respectfully) that she is going to move out of what amounts to a visual embrace.

A mother tells me that her son responds very well to her using his body language, apart from one gesture. When he holds up his hands over his chest, he is very upset if she does the same. I suggest to her that, rather than simply never using this gesture, one might respond to it by standing away, moving her hands to a similar position but then turning them so her palms face him and very gently lowering them to a position of being flat on a table, a gesture signifying acceptance of his discomfort.

In both these cases we are not just capping what a person says but using gestures instead of words to further the conversation. The way we move is analogous to the tone of our voice in speech. Just as how our partners move indicates how they feel, how we move tells them about us. We need to use our bodies to convey our humour, pleasure, surprise, withdrawal, interest and understanding.

Imitation, mimicking and free-flowing conversation

To move a conversation on, Gunnar Vege uses 'delayed imitation' to further sensory memories he calls 'traces'. In a fascinating film we watch him take Ingerid, a blind-deaf girl, to the seaside. They sit together on a floating pier, so she feels the transmitted lapping movement of the waves. He introduces her to a little crab which they hold together and let it scuttle up her arm. This is a unique sensory experience, not easily confused with similar events. The following day he takes her again, recreating the ambience but without the crab. He tickles her palm with his fingers and starts up her arm, holding the gesture before completion. She quickly picks up his intent and her left hand scuttles up her arm. She is clearly remembering the physical sensations of the previous day and in essence she and Gunnar are having a delayed conversation about an event they enjoyed together (Vege 2006).

To return to Ron who reversed his baseball cap when I used his sounds to talk to him during a workshop. His mother feels the difference is one of relationship. She tells me that after seeing him respond so vividly at the workshop, she and her husband tried answering his sounds when they got home. At first they were concerned about feeling silly and whether or not they were mimicking him. But she said: 'The worry fell away when we found he responded. It brought out the person in him and his confidence grew as he was taken seriously. He spent more time inter-acting with us.' Although he did not use words, she told me it was as if he was saying, 'Hello, Mum, how are you?' She continued:

> It made a difference to our relationship. Before, I felt as if I was just a function – there to provide his needs. That changed as he made me feel a person for him rather than just a provider. Now he wanted to know me and I wanted to know him. Before, I looked at his behaviour, now I see the person.

And his behaviour has changed. Three years ago, provision for Ron was discussed in terms of the need for a secure unit. Having been able to return to school, plans are now afoot for him to continue supported education at college.

Even when our partner is on the autistic spectrum we find to our surprise that, whereas under conditions which are user-friendly for the neurotypical brain but are perceived as threatening by our partners, if we are using gestures based on their language they often prove adept at inter-preting our feelings.

In trying to understand what it is that is actually happening when we talk to our partner through Intensive Interaction, there is a problem with the use of the word 'imitation'. We need to explore this, since in the litera-ture it is used in several different ways. In a fascinating paper on how mothers share feeling-states with their infants, Jonsson *et al.* (2001) dis-tinguish between imitation as 'the mimicking of facial expressions, movements and vocalisations using the same modality as the initiated behaviour' and 'affective attunement', 'which involves an alternative modality, or if the same modality is used, there is a clear affective emphasis'. (In the former case the mother simply copies exactly what the infant does, but in the latter she might echo a stretch movement with a sound that reflected the effort put into the movement, 'Ooo-ooh', echoing how the action feels through rhythm and sound.)

One way of looking at this is to regard both imitation and affective attunement as parts of a courtship ritual that brings to bear all the skills necessary for establishing relationship. This also includes testing boundaries, referring back (letting our partner know we are interested in what they are thinking), offering and exploring ideas and objects that we hope may be of mutual interest, teasing within empathetic boundaries, humour and sharing; anything that attracts and binds us together – and with all the security *that* brings, deliver the feeling of emotional congruence, of being at one with each other. Now we have an ally with whom to face up to the world and in whose company we can explore new horizons. In this shared playground we explore and define 'self' and 'other' (or 'me' and 'not me' as Geraint Ephraim called it in a personal communication). As an interaction it is the most fundamental conversation we shall ever have.

We have come a long way from imitation as mimicking, and it is a word I am reluctant to use because, in spite of the amazing part it has played in the development of our capacity to relate, many of us will associate it with schoolyard mockery. In this context it is a term of disrespect, where the intention is to use the 'victim' as an object for self-aggrandizement. These negative associations go some way towards explaining why care providers have suspected that what we are about when we use Intensive Interaction is in some way demeaning. But as I have already indicated, to find the true value of imitation we have to return to our infancy. It is here that we learn that it is the gateway to communication. It is on our mother's lap, through her imitation and confirmation of our initiatives that we all first learn about ourselves. In this context, imitation is creative and open-ended.

Humour

In her book *Feeling Other Minds*, Vasu Reddy (2006) emphasizes that from the beginning humour is a social event. Even if I see something which makes me laugh on my own, my first instinct is that it will be fun to tell so and so. There is added value in the sharing.

This is where humour comes in. For example, it can relieve stress. Making a joke of things can alleviate what is otherwise a distressing and uncomfortable situation, bring the participants together with a feeling of mutual support. So if we want to get to know each other, we do this by offering things which we think will interest our potential partner, in particular those things we think they will find funny, that will capture their attention in a way that will make them want to spend more time with us. This is where humour comes in. For example it can relieve stress. Making a joke of things can alleviate what is otherwise a distressing and uncomfortable situation, bringing the participants together with a feeling of mutual support.

A small plane taxis out to the apron and waits for take-off. It is already three hours delayed because snow has closed runways. It is also uncomfortable, all strangers packed together. The captain informs his passengers that there will be a further long delay as they have now missed their place in the de-icing queue. The man by the window sighs and says, 'We may be here all night.' The woman beside him turns to him and says, 'Don't worry, in half-an-hour I shall introduce myself.' They laugh together. This small joke opened up opportunities and a new shared perspective. What had appeared to be a vista of endless boredom, discomfort and some anxiety took on a different perspective, an opportunity to explore, an invitation to togetherness. It is the unexpected element of this exchange, the absurd qualification, the 'not now but later' which gives their joke a humorous twist and opens the way out of (in this case) a rather depressing situation. Tension is released and the spirit lifted – here is an ally and things really looked a little better.

When he was asked how he thought of ideas for his cartoons in a daily newspaper, the cartoonist 'Matt' said that in a way it was easy, it was just a matter of putting together two apparently unassociated topical ideas. From our point of view, humour is a discontinuity in expectation, a jolt which 'tickles our fancy', grabs our attention. There is a distinction between expectation and actualization. We are led into assumption of one thing but get another or see it in a different light.

Humour is the ladder we can use to climb out of ourselves. We also use it to test affinity, to find out if our partner is 'one of us', someone who will react in a way that we can predict if events turn out to be difficult. It not only promotes relationship but is also the gauge we can use to test this.

Comparisons suggest that children on the autistic spectrum do not use this social skill in the way that it is used by Down's syndrome or neurotypical children (Reddy *et al.* 2002). I should suggest that this is not always so. Like a number of things that are said about people on the spectrum (such as their inability to generalize) it depends partly on the 'currency' of the joke – how it is put – and also partly on the subject. Here is a friend who is on the autistic spectrum talking about jokes:

> Jokes are the source of lightness of heart. I think autism is often very good at jokes. It is very evident at conferences and splits the autistic firmly from the non-autistic; autistic humour is very allusive, though very literal and self-aware. It is almost a defining feature – often allusive to something that only the spectrum people will have noticed. They therefore all understand and laugh, the others remain baffled and one can't explain what is funny without huge labour. So it is about language and whose the language is.

Ros Blackburn, who is on the autistic spectrum, is what she herself calls a 'speak-freak', a linguistic savant. She has a passion for words and, in spite of her autism (or perhaps in her case, because of it), is a magnificent speaker. Her humour is dispassionate and literal. For example, when told that she was now regarded as a 'consumer' rather than a 'patient' at her doctor's surgery, she remarked that although she had once bitten a doctor, she had never eaten a whole one.

I am not sure that this makes it any different to a neurotypical sense of humour since much of this is also allusive rather than explicit, it is more about sharing the subtext, the underlying message. You either get it or you don't. It is so easy (and sometimes humiliating and excluding) not to get a joke – or to tell one and it falls flat on its face because the teller and the listener are not sharing common ground. Then we say that the other has no sense of humour, when what we mean is we cannot understand their jokes, they do not make sense to us, a defence mechanism: better to reject them, rather than feel rejected.

Before moving on, I want to explore this further through two further examples. In the first, I am the partner who is introducing an unexpected element. In the second, it is my partner who quite deliberately brings humour into our interaction.

Phil, who is on the autistic spectrum, is extremely disturbed. He comes in to the Resource Centre he attends at the beginning of the day, finds himself a magazine, switches on his favourite tape and sits down in a secluded corner. Effectively he is cutting himself off from any untoward stimuli and can just about cope unless he is disturbed. If this happens, he screams and bites himself. This screaming can go on for an hour or so – and so far no way has been found of calming him down. I suggest to his support partner that he also get a magazine and sit near him turning the pages when he does. Two things emerge. Phil enjoys pictures of dogs, and when he is enjoying himself he slaps his knee. Sitting on the other side of the table, when he finds a dog picture, I bark. Phil smiles. We repeat this several times, but next time I respond, instead of barking I try a miaow. This time he looks at me, giggles and slaps his leg and then really laughs loudly. Sharing my fooling-about joke we are drawn into joint laughter.

In the second episode I am working with a man whose behaviour is so distressed and potentially violent that he needs four people to oversee him at any one time. They stay in one half of the room and he stays in the other. The activity he focuses on is to scribble. I sit at a table and pick up my pen and scribble too. He comes over to see what I am doing, sits down and we share the activity, when he scribbles, I scribble. He begins to smile and after a few minutes, gives me a mischievous look and quite deliberately turns and scribbles on the table. He then turns back to me, laughing at me with a look on his face which says, 'What are you going to do about that?' (the table did not matter, it was old and worn out). I look at him and laugh and shrug my shoulders and say, 'I can't do that' and we laugh together. We stop feeling afraid of each other – he is my friend with whom I have shared a joke.

Intimacy, trust and humour are part of a package. In both these episodes, one partner is pushing the boundaries of relationship by adding an unexpected element to our interaction and referring back to their partner to see if they will also find it funny. As I have already suggested, it can almost be regarded as a courtship ritual, when, in our desire to win friends and allies we are showing off, parading our wares and particularly, in running the risk of rejection, allowing ourselves to be momentarily vulnerable. When our eyes meet they say, I know what you are doing and I find it funny too. In sharing each other's quirky sense of humour there is, at least until we have learned the limits of each other's territory, a sense of relief when we find that we share the same landscape. As we learn what we have in common, we also see it through new eyes, eyes that we trust to extend the vision of our own horizons.

At the end of the first day I worked with Andy, during which time he had moved from self-stimulation (lost in an inner language of sounds and waving arms) to one of lively interaction (smiling and referring back to us), his communication partner asked if he might sit beside him. Andy's response was to get up and plonk himself firmly in the requested chair, look up at his partner and laugh at him. We laughed with him, delighted at the appearance of his new-found self-confidence. There was no mistake, he was quite deliberately teasing his partner. This may seem a little thing, but for Andy this was an immense step, an empowerment and indication of himself in relation to others.

Laugh and the world laughs with you. But only if everything is going your way. Imagine the opposite scenario, one in which Andy's foray into teasing is rejected and he is firmly moved back to the sofa which is where he is expected to sit. This would have been an assault on who he is, his dignity and worth. We have to be extremely careful not to crush but rather to pick up and particularly to show people that we value their pleasure. This is what empowerment is about – in showing people that we enjoy their company we leave them feeling better about themselves.

Imitation as a departure platform

The second difficulty I have with the word imitation is that although it describes the activity on which Intensive Interaction is based, it is misleading as an attitude, since it is something 'I do to you' or 'you do to me', rather than a journey we share.

Looked at in this context, Intensive Interaction is about developing relationships in a way which uses imitation – but where imitation is not an end in itself. Rather we should think of it as a departure platform from which Intensive Interaction leaves. There are a number of possible routes – and any number of destinations. One can take the slow or fast train but we need to start from the correct platform (something the brain recognizes as significant, part of its repertoire). The answer to the question of 'Where shall we go today?' is up for negotiation.

It really is important to understand this, because when imitation is used on its own, it can hit the buffers: 'habituation' is where the brain learns to expect a particular response, gets it and, to put it simply, loses interest. It is no longer a signal which is worth attending to. At this stage both partners get into a rut and the whole interaction loses its vitality.

We now know that our brains contain nerve cells, mirror neurons, which recognize when they are presented with an action from their own repertoire. So at first I may need to copy what my partner is doing exactly, so that they recognize their own signals and their attention is gathered. Gradually, as I become more fluent in the elements of their internal conversation, I will respond with small differences, alternating with their initiatives and answering rather than copying, as in normal dialogue. For example, I may put together more than one of their elements in unfamiliar juxtaposition. The brain recognizes its own language but is jolted by the sudden twist – the unforeseen 'stranger' popping up within the familiar context of its own language. The brain is intrigued, placed on alert by an unanticipated factor embedded within what it had expected.

A child is sitting in a pool scooping the water up to her face. Her communication partner responds to this, at first by repeating what she is doing, but then by smacking the surface of the water, which makes a completely different sound. Up until now the child has simply been aware of her partner's actions, but as soon as she hears the different sound she turns immediately to him, smiling. Her attention has moved from awareness of to interactive engagement. Suddenly there is something even more interesting apart from her self-stimulatory activity. (As she turns round, he needs to smack the water again with a slightly different rhythm, to both confirm but also to intrigue and further lure her interest.)

Relating to the effectiveness in communication of 'difference', in her fascinating book on the development of the human voice, Anne Karpf (2006) cites the findings of Joseph Jaffe and others in a study of the development of attachment in babies. When attachment between mothers and babies is measured at twelve months, it appears to be directly related to the patterns of vocal rhythm between mothers and their four-month-old infants – but not quite in the way that might have been anticipated. At twelve months, babies who at four months had been in a badly rhythmically coordinated pair were not well attached, but, unexpectedly, so also were infants in the most rhythmically synchronized pairs.

> The most secure infants occupied a middle position, with space for flexibility and variation. Their mothers provided enough regularity of vocal rhythm and tempo to allow them to predict the pace and shape of their interaction but also variability and novelty to be exciting. As a result the mid-range pairs could be playful with each other. (Jaffe *et al.* 2001)

Flexibility (within the boundaries of our repertoire) is intriguing, it leads us on so that our attention hardens to engagement. We begin to be really interested in each other.

The time taken for the penny to drop ('if I do something, I will get an answer') varies. Although a colleague told me that with one partner with whom he interacted, it had taken a year to make the connection – an incredible tribute to his persistence, normally this is made extremely quickly. In my experience, twenty minutes is a long time. For example the report on a child (who was very disturbed) I was handed on arrival said that imitation had been tried with her and had been unsuccessful. But we do not always get it quite right, so I tried again to see if I could find a more successful approach. I met her after lunch when she was in her room on her bed and I was standing outside. When she made a sound, I responded without thinking. Although she could not see me since I was hidden behind another person, she leapt from her bed, found me, grabbed my hand and pulled me over to sit beside her. Just one sound was enough to bring her, a profoundly autistic child, to a stranger. It was that important to her. We 'talked' using her sounds for about quarter of an hour. Having demonstrated to her support partners how to interact, it was I who had to end our delightful conversation since I had to visit someone else.

This is not unique. Quite often the link is almost instantaneous, that is as soon as we manage to isolate the behaviour which the brain recognizes as significant (rather than one that our partner is using to protect them-selves). It really is a matter of trial and error and building off the feedback offered by our partner's responses. Even if this is negative, it helps define the boundaries of possibility. If I am rejected, I move away and use my body language to ask the question 'Is this better?', opening my arms and hands and placing the head to one side. Indications are that whatever the time taken, the sequence of events is the same, a move from isolation to enjoyment of relationship.

At this stage, particularly if they feel the mutual interest flagging, people will sometimes say, 'What do I do next?' This is completely to mis-understand the nature of the interaction, which needs to be looked at as a means rather than an end. Using our body language to answer theirs, we explore how each other feels. It is a tool for developing relationship, incorporating all the structures of conversation, such as pauses and referring back. Using it gives a person who is non-verbal access to a way of expressing themselves and also to having their feelings validated. This is what equality and valuing a person is about. I value you, not with an aim to improving you – but as you are. Once they understand that they now have a way of expressing their feelings which both they and their partners understand, that both are playing the same game by the same rules – and these rules include the possibility of flexible innovation, they frequently respond with a kind of joyful and expanding curiosity.

Play and games

At this point I want to go back to the issue of the language we use and the way we think about each other. For a long time I have gone along with the idea that when we speak of 'play' and 'games' in conjunction with work with adults, we are in some way lacking respect for them and treating them as children. This oversimplification arises from the quite proper desire to treat people with consideration for their intrinsic value as grown-up individuals, but at the same time it suggests that there is a fault line between childhood and adulthood.

'Play' has a number of associations, a surprising proportion of which are negative, for example, she's 'playing up', 'playing the fool', 'playing hard to get', 'playing away', 'playing fast and loose', or we 'play down' possible consequences in order to conceal them, a byproduct of spin. It is as if somehow, we who are grown up are ashamed of our childish ways. Looking back we see that we were naïve. Now that we know better we can invent rules to protect ourselves from our own vulnerability. Sticking to the rules, if we lose we can fall back on being 'good losers', 'it's only a game'. As adults we disguise our games as 'sport' or 'collecting'.

But we continue to behave as if 'play' is part of our regrettable past, demeaning, only tolerable if it is called a 'leisure activity', a rest from the serious business of adult work. Such a prospect overlooks the continuity of what it is to be a person grown out of the child, and bars the doorway to creativity.

And in the *New Oxford Dictionary*, there is a startling omission – there is no mention of 'playing with ideas' where the mind is allowed to wander without maps through 'what-if' corridors, placing images in unusual juxtaposition, trying out metaphors, exploring feelings – and moving beyond ourselves, to test out and share these thoughts and discoveries with others.

We have learned and continue to learn who we are through sharing with others. To respect a person is to open up ourselves emotionally alongside them as they are – and not as we feel they ought to be. So *what* we do with them, the precise activity, is not so important as finding ways of being with each other. Joining in their flicking string activity may not be regarded as a productive and age appropriate occupation in itself but the function of play and games is as a vehicle for interaction. We learn to have fun with each other by using our interactions in a playful manner, in a mode that is meaningful for them. We explore what is valuable to our partners and confirm it – and learning to trust ourselves to our partners, offer to them what we value, sharing our emotional states. It is through relearning to value the child in ourselves and in others that we learn what it is to be truly human: child or adult, we all play games with each other. By exploring what we enjoy with others we come to know 'other which is not ourselves'. We test our boundaries and are enriched by our experience of their self. We make friends; and in a difficult world, friends make life worth living.

However, if we are going to use the concept of 'play' and 'games' I find I need to distinguish between play, which is open-ended and 'games', which have structure and rules ('this is what we do'). To some extent rules are a protection against placing ourselves in a position of vulnerability. The trouble is that games can become an end in themselves, and unfortunately there are practitioners of Intensive Interaction who see it in this light. Their interactions become mechanical, closed-ended instead of open and full of possibility.

If we are going to explore as deeply as possible the emotional world of our partner, it is leaving the self totally open that allows the emergence and exploration of new possibilities, carrying us beyond the boundaries of our own limited territories and around the next corner. If we leave ourselves open to 'affective teasing', by which I mean a delicate probing of 'Where will this lead us next?', we find ourselves on a journey into a shared and often joyful venture into the unknown. It is how we grow.

Alienation and intimacy

I try and discourage people from using the terms 'mimicry', 'mirroring', 'imitation' and even 'copying', since they give the idea of an interaction that is closed-ended. In workshops, people sometimes even ask what is the actual difference between these and 'response' and 'answering'.

Not long ago, I watched an intervention that answered this question for me, both literally and metaphorically. Jack is a totally solitary young man with autism, amiable but with a slightly puzzled look, in his own world much of the time. He loves roller-blading and is extremely good at this, gliding effortlessly round a large tarmac space the size of two tennis courts at the back of the house. His support partner, Pete, finds it difficult to keep up with him.

Jack takes off and Pete follows him, waving his arms as Jack does. Jack smiles. He notices Pete but the interaction only really gets going when we introduce a tube, which I suggest that Pete offers Jack to see if he will hold the other end. Jack takes the proffered end and they start to glide round together, their bodies moving in unison as they synchronize and relax into each other's movements. Soon it seems as if Pete is no longer thinking about what he has to do, their responses to each other are totally attuned, like a tango, where each partner makes different movements but in relation to the other, complementing their partner. Jack puts his head close to Pete's and gazes at him while they continue to skate.

Pete tires first and comes to sit on the wall. Jack follows him over and tugs at his sleeve. Now he wants to skate with Pete rather than on his own. This time, Jack holds the tube with one hand, his other rests on Pete's arm. Who is pulling whom? And does it matter? At the end, Jack comes and stands close to Pete. There is a prolonged interval of close gaze and communication.

The day that we learn to dance is not, as one might expect, the day when we finally master the movements but rather the day we let go of ourselves. What had happened between Jack and Pete was that Pete had moved from a slightly self-conscious 'I do what he does' to free-flow, where both he and Jack are literally at one, in harmony, joined in this case by a cardboard tube but also by intention and attention, each totally focused in their partner. Jack's face was radiant. They had moved beyond imitation and copying to engagement and intimacy.

Imitation on its own is too limiting. We have to surrender any idea of schedule and structure and abandon ourselves, not just copying sounds and movements but, more fundamentally, opening ourselves to the tempo and rhythms of our partners.

People who are not used to using body language are quite often shocked by the degree of intimacy which it brings, especially with people on the autistic spectrum, with whom current theory suggests one might not expect to develop quite such deep mutual attentiveness and close relationship. It is quite normal for a session to end in a warm hug accompanied by the feeling that one's partner is experiencing an immense sense of relief at being able to communicate, at actually finding some way of being in touch which does not threaten to overwhelm them.

Feeling helpless or silly

When I talked to a support partner about how it felt to start using our partner's body language, she said that for her, one of the main difficulties was actually remembering to do it. We are so locked into our dominant mode of communication that we have to make a real effort to switch to thinking about how our partner is communicating. This does not necessarily come naturally – we have to think about what we are doing, not always easy, especially in crisis situations. Most people say that once through the first fortnight, it becomes second nature. It is starting that is the hard bit.

But in fact we are using body language all the time. It is difficult to convey sounds which are not words in print, but the following may give some idea of how we use such mini-communications to support our inter-actions all the time, particularly to convey and transmit how we feel, expressions both of our own feelings and those of attention, presence, solidarity and empathy with others. The different inflexions are quite subtle.

- We nod our heads, 'Ah', to agree.
- We lift our voices at the end of a sound to make a query, 'Ah-Ah?'.
- We recoil in disgust, 'Eeergh'.
- We shake our heads to disagree and say 'Er-Er'.
- When we are not sure we might say 'Mmm'.
- We say 'Ooch!' followed by an intake of breath to sympathize if someone is describing something painful.
- We say 'Ooh!' to express surprise.

All these are ways we can align ourselves empathetically with our partner.

However when we do start to use Intensive Interaction, we may have a feeling of helplessness or even panic: we look round for help, what ought I to be doing, what are the rules here? We want reassurance that we are doing it right. What we have to learn is that the only person who can help us is our partner. This is our place of reference, this is the only place where we can learn how to interact.

Our partner is our teacher. And if we find ourselves doing things which we feel are silly, what we are actually thinking is that what our partners are doing is silly, that their attempts to communicate in the only ways open to them are in some way beneath our dignity – and also, that if other people see us being what we feel is silly it will devalue us in their eyes. When we feel silly it is actually the fear of looking silly which is the problem, that we shall look ridiculous in the eyes of our peers and this will lead them to reject us.

We need to re-evaluate our premise and refocus our attention, understanding the value and courage of our partners whose efforts to get in touch with us we have ignored to the point where it has no longer seemed worth trying. We must refocus away from what we think those around us are feeling about us and into the world of our partner, giving them intimate attention.

Such a shift is evident in a conversation with a family member who is talking about their changing attitude to her foster sister's sounds after they had started using Intensive Interaction. Jemma has severe cerebral palsy and is non-verbal.

> We had always used Jemma's silly noises to make her laugh…and quite disrespectfully called them silly noises – but they were not silly, they were Jemma's way of communicating and we had to learn to use them constructively. (Quoted in Caldwell and Stevens 2005)

And Ron's mother said that when she and her husband used Intensive Interaction, they at first felt silly, but this soon passed when they realized how pleased he was at his new-found ability to communicate.

As in any conversation, we need to be flexible and work from our partner's initiatives as they happen, and not according to some pre-planned worksheet, otherwise the message we send our partners by our lack of timely response is that we are not interested in what they are saying, we are not listening to them, we are simply pursuing our own line of thought without respect for them or interest in how they feel.

And this really brings us to the heart of how we feel about the people with whom we are engaged. We need to ask ourselves if we truly value them as they are, or are we paying lip service to the ideals of respect?

A team approach

Because the use of body language is so effective and very quickly brings about behavioural change, it is important that it is a joint approach, not just one that takes place with one person. Our partner needs to learn that it is possible and helpful and fun to communicate with the outside world in general rather than with one person, so that they begin to perceive their environment as user-friendly rather than incomprehensible and/or hostile. And we need to share our increasing skills with all those involved with the child or adult, not just care staff but parents, friends and teachers. Video can be extremely helpful, not only so that we can pick up the bits in our own practice but also in showing to others the best ways to relate.

To summarize, there is more to using body language than just imitation. Far from being a superficial mimicry of sounds and movements, what it does is to confirm the internal messaging of a person, it helps them to know who they are and in doing so also imparts value to who and what they are. From our point of view, observation of body language helps us to interpret the complexity of a brain's manoeuvres to make sense of its world of misinterpretation and psychological pain. Our aim is to shift our partner's attention from retreat to the inner world (and its sometimes desperate attempts to reduce over-stimulation by focus on repetitive behaviour, withdrawal or aggression) and refocus it in positive engagement with the outside world both through modification of the environment and use of empathy and a common language.

To do this, if we are the skilled partner working with someone on the autistic spectrum, we may, as Melanie Nind indicates,

> have to learn to develop our intuitive powers as interactive part-
> ners but also learn to unpick our intuitions and respond and initi-
> ate in a way that may fall outside of, or run counter to our normal
> intuitive approach. (Nind and Powell 2000)

There are times when the effects of using a person's body language are so dramatic that the outcome can seem almost miraculous. Using their own language to divert their focus from the inner to the outer world helps them to feel secure instead of afraid. Lowering the stress level enables the brain to function better (as signified by the ability to generalize, understand more speech and sometimes start to use speech themselves), and they are able to focus on the outside world and connect with it better.

But we also do need a dual approach: at the same time as establishing a common language and using it as a route to how a person feels, we have to look at what it is that is upsetting and stressing our partner. (In the case of autism, a detailed account of the underlying triggers of hypersensitivity to sensory stimuli will be found in Caldwell 2000a, 2000b, 2002a, 2006 and Gillingham 1995.)

To illustrate the need to keep a lookout for possible sensory hypersensitivities I want to return to Nick and his Hallowe'en wizard's paper hat. Apart from successful work with his movements and sounds, the manner in which he is pulling down the broad black brim suggests that while this may just be a generalized retreat from over-stimulation, a 'stop-the-world-I-want-to-get-off' strategy, there is also the possibility that, like many people on the spectrum, he is hypersensitive to light. (Others with a similar difficulty will hide their eyes under their hands, pull clothes over their heads and in bright light, screw up their eyes. Some respond to interaction much better in dimmer or certain colours of light, since under these conditions it is easier for the brain to process incoming signals.) Not only do we have to establish the communication link but we also need to reduce the underlying factors that are responsible for his pain and distress.

Whatever approach is used, all have to answer one question, '*Is it working?*' Is it enabling this person to live a life that is more peaceful, more fulfilling and more fun? What seems strange to those of us who are using Intensive Interaction so successfully is that if, as we are claiming, it is so effective, why are we not all doing it?

Resistance to using approaches based on imitation and body language

There are still pockets of resistance to implementation, some of them obvious, some of them less so.

The first reason must be that at the time Intensive Interaction was introduced under its previous name of 'Augmented Mothering' the attention of providing authorities was very much focused on 'normalization' and 'age appropriateness'. While these have an important role to play they do not address the problem of people whose sensory interpretation of the reality we share differs from our interpretation of normality. At the same time, the attention of many psychologists was focused on the approach known as Behavioural Modification, which is actually a form of control, however benign. Rewarding good behaviour and ignoring, rejecting or 'punishing' negative behaviour may work for some people, but for others it simply increases their stress level. In particular, it can run the risk of encouraging our partners to reject their 'bad' feelings, which are then split off and buried or projected. Either way, being unable to own one's own feelings can lead to explosive outbursts of violence later on in life. When we come to meet Sandra in Chapter 12 we shall see how she has learned different voices to express different parts of her personality and how the struggle to contain her rejected bad bits leads her to aggression.

Another reason for the failure of Intensive Interaction to take off immediately is that when the hospitals for people with learning disability closed, some of the new community homes were staffed by people whose attitudes were extremely entrenched. Unfortunately, these were often the homes offered to the most 'difficult' residents, such people having been the least easy to resettle – and the more forward-looking staff having moved out first. Some of these older staff felt they had a lifetime's experience of knowing how to control behaviour and saw no reason to alter their ways. They could not put aside their defences since they were afraid of following the lead of someone they fundamentally did not trust. They saw the unknown as a threat rather than an opportunity. There was an even deeper fear – 'If I let go, shall I be able to get back?' – setting the pattern for newer younger staff who joined later.

When the people they are caring for are aggressive, support staff may see the solution in terms of increased numbers to control behaviour, rather than enquiring into the roots of the behaviour. I am still being invited to see clients where staff feel they cannot manage on a four-to-one basis and want to increase the number present at any one time to five. In such cases as these, one has to ask whether the concern expressed is on the basis of cost, or concern that there just may be an error in practice?

And finally, there is the problem that some people say that when they use their partner's body language they feel silly – silly in the sense that other people will laugh at them. While it may sound overdramatic in this context, rejection by our group is a very serious business since, in biological terms, it can lead to death. Belonging is one of the great imperatives of survival and we devote much of our lives struggling to win allies. But the corollary of this is to say that our partners are less valuable than our peers. While this may be true if judged on the basis of whether they can support us, it does not detract from their intrinsic worth as individuals. To be able to say to someone 'You are important to me' is to liberate them and ourselves from the constraints of isolation. If this is what we are trying to say, why don't we just get on with it?

It takes time for ideas to filter through and become common currency, but Intensive Interaction has been around for a long time and is now a part of some university degree and training packages. But the problem is that it is so simple that it's hard to believe that we would not already have thought of it if it was a viable approach. And the theoretical world demands proof, clinical trials and long-term studies. Before going on to look at the evidence of its effectiveness, the next chapter will take a look in more detail at what we think we are trying to do when we use non-verbal communication.

5

What Are We Trying to Do?

Learning to listen

This reaches deeper than just what we are trying to do with our partners into what we think is really valuable about being a human being. What is it in this strange and often terrible world that makes it worth while? In the light of the title of this book, *From Isolation to Intimacy*, what is it we really want for the people for whom we work? The answer to this question is not as simple as it seems. Consideration suggests that what many of us really desire is that 'disability' would go away and that people should be able to perform on their own in our world. In effect, we are valuing independence above interdependence, in the sense that seeing them dependent on us we miss what it is that we have to learn from them as people. This is not to say that the disability in itself has value, but it most emphatically does say that a person's difference does not alter their essential worth.

So how can we convey worth? Think about communication. First of all there is the casual greeting. Walk down our village street and almost everyone you meet, regardless of whether or not you know each other well, will look at you and say, 'Morning', 'Hello' or if it's a particularly sunny day, 'Grand day isn't it?' These passing exchanges are a form of social reassurance, of grooming. If you don't believe this, just recall what happens if you smile and say 'Hello' and someone fails to respond, looks right through you. You will feel momentarily rejected and possibly mutter to yourself 'Didn't think much of them anyway' or 'Must be a stranger'. What you are doing is internally rejecting them in order to right the balance in yourself.

These small pleasantries are an important use of language, and their absence is one of the downsides of urban living. They tell us who we are, that we are part of the tribe even if remotely connected, not excluded. And we can use this with our non-verbal partners by greeting them in language that they recognize and is non-threatening (in the sense that it does not contribute to overload) each time we pass by. Every time we do this we are acknowledging them, offering inclusion and reassurance, and also in the case of those who are very withdrawn, shifting their attention from their inner world to our shared world that exists outside themselves. If they can find a way of making sense of their external environment, they do not have to turn in on themselves, listening to their own repetitive behaviour. A teacher suggested we call this process, 'top-up', a drip-feed process redirecting the brain from chaos to coherence. We might think of it as being able to follow cat's-eyes down the middle of the road at night. In the darkness, we know where we are.

A child shuts herself in her room and watches TV. When she comes out, she is overloaded and about to have an outburst. There are two alternative scenarios. In the first, when she sees people moving about, it adds to the already brimming over unprocessed stimuli she is trying to deal with and tips her into fragmentation: everything in her brain breaks up, she goes into melt-down. Alternatively, when she opens the door, someone greets her with a familiar sound, a common link, a part of her personal repertoire which her brain can take on board and on which she can focus when the rest of her sensory world is swirling away. This is non-threatening, and the rising tide of her stress goes into reverse and she calms down.

When it comes to conversation, if we listen to ourselves when we talk, we find that we spend quite a lot of time pushing our own agenda. One of the differences between this and when we are using non-verbal language with our partners is a shift of emphasis from 'my thrust' to attention to your responses.

So, perhaps it would help if we looked at the question 'What are we trying to do?' the other way round. What we are not trying to do, at least directly, is to change our partners (although we may be hoping to provide conditions in which they will feel valued and consequently grow in confidence). Primarily, however, what we are about is finding out who they are and how they feel and promoting a feeling of well-being. Our interactions are about being present, not weighted to a possible future – this is where we need to be, here, with our partner, now, accepting them and as they are, understanding rather than rejecting those bits that do not fit into our plan. In fact a conditional valuation, 'I will love you if you are *not* the same as you are now', is an absurdity, a non sequitur that conveys the message 'As you are, you are not good enough for me'.

(To swap sides for a minute – we can hardly grow in self-confidence if we live in the shadow of expectations that we are unable to meet. And yet this is precisely what is happening every time we try to communicate in the only way we know how. You take no notice of our grunts, sighs, screams and movements – so we turn inwards on ourselves, at least there is someone here who will listen.)

'So when I practise, I am going to listen, to be present to you with all my senses tuned in to your presence, so that in this intimate attention we can become in each other, you in me and I in you, here.' This sort of language brings us to a different place than 'I observed what she was doing and then copied her.' It speaks of an internal awareness which has a primal feel about it. I have put aside cognition and interpretation and have become aware of you through unprocessed sensation. I watch the pages of your feeling turn.

We are at a workshop and the audience includes some people with learning disability and a woman with Asperger's syndrome. She wants to know the personal details of everyone in the room, questioning to the point where the rest of the audience is becoming restless and it has become impossible to continue. She is driven by her exponential desire. Time to lay down a boundary – but as I do so I catch the glimmer of the struggle in her eyes as she wrestles with the contraflow in her brain – 'I have to know/I can't know' – competing for attention. At this point I am aware not just of my own dilemma (how to keep the dynamic of the workshop in process) but also of her pain. Such eyeball exchange realizes itself in my flesh, I feel it: very powerful. It tells me how she is in her world. As we re-emerge into the cognitive world, I wonder fleetingly what we have lost when we learned to speak?

Lowering stress

A child with Down's syndrome cannot sleep. He wakes frequently and his mother says he 'growls'. Having attended a workshop on the use of body language, when he wakes on the following night, his mother responds to his sounds with soft growly noises. He relaxes at once, curls up and goes back to sleep.

But before we look at how well the use of body language works, we need to understand what it is trying to do. Commenting on this, Barber (2006) points out from the educational point of view that while it does not directly improve academic levels, this is not what it sets out to accomplish. What it does do, often dramatically, is to improve the ability to relate, the desire to communicate, while simultaneously reducing distressed behaviour. My own experience in practice with non-verbal children and adults, both those with multiple disability and those on the autistic spectrum, is that once the person understands they will always receive a response to their initiatives, the brain becomes less stressed. The external sign of this is a relaxation of the facial muscles.

Bearing in mind the sensory confusion experienced by people on the autistic spectrum, perhaps it is helpful to think of Intensive Interaction, using our partner's body language, as a navigational aid such as the beacons or lights that guide a boat into safe harbour at night. Using signals the brain recognizes, because they are part of their familiar repertoire, gives their brain a point of reference, a mark on which to home in, not only in the spatial but also in the temporal sense, letting them know what is going on. At this stage it appears that the brain processes begin to operate more effectively. Just as an example, far from being absent in people on the autistic spectrum, the ability to generalize appears to be active, even if it presents at a low level, such as moving from one mode of interaction to another and referring back to see what their partner will make of the change in response.

('I know if I flick my string you will answer by flicking yours, how about if I bang the sink?')

In other words, the partner is generalizing in order to test the process. It does seem that (particularly in the urgent search for understanding of the condition of autism) one of the problems is that researchers may fail to recognize processes because they pitch the cognitive demands of their investigations in the wrong direction: failure to understand the task at a cognitive level leading to a belief that the process is in itself faulty. Somehow we have to learn to frame experimental procedures within the personal language of the person involved.

Another outcome for people on the autistic spectrum is that as their stress level drains away, they are more able to process incoming information and speech is more easily unscrambled. They may begin to understand quite complex sentences with dependent clauses. For example, at the end of a session of Intensive Interaction, a woman with ASD who did not appear to make any connections at all through speech was able to respond immediately to 'If I had been twisting my hair like this, I should want to brush my hair – and if I wanted to brush my hair, I should put my hairbrush on the bed' by slamming her brush on the quilt ('If I wanted to do X, I should do Y first').

And depending on the level of disability, appropriate speech may develop. This is particularly dramatic in adults. In children, even though they may have shown no signs of speech previously, one might argue that it was simply a matter of delayed development, whereas to witness the arrival of speech in a man of twenty-three who has been effectively non-verbal until now is amazing. In a privately videoed session of work with Pranve, discussed in *Finding You Finding Me*, he moves from making very small sounds to a louder triplet which resolves as 'Where's Charlene?', the only thing he has been known to say previously. Four hours later he is clearly and loudly singing, 'Baa Baa Black Sheep' much to the astonishment of his mother and father and also the speech therapist who has been present throughout. The interesting thing about this progression is that he produces the tune some time before he manages to organize the words. The struggle to do so is clearly visible on his face, to the extent that his chin wobbles with the effort to articulate them. He knows what he wants to do before he can frame it. During this process he continually refers back to me to see what I am making of his efforts.

At a deeper level, the use of a person's body language appears to affect the whole capacity to process incoming information. To understand the consequences of lowering stress levels in people with autism, I want to look at a discussion on 'self-consciousness' by Vasu Reddy on infant and child development, *Feeling Other Minds* (Reddy 2006), in particular the 'two-sides-of-a-coin' self-conscious behaviours of 'shyness' and 'showing off'. The argument here is not about autism as such, but rather about the age at which infants develop their awareness of what we term 'self' – but it goes on to compare the behaviour of children without autism to those on the spectrum.

To begin with shyness, Vasu Reddy records its body language in a very powerful way, describing this as lowering the visibility of self – just as to 'show off' is to raise the profile of self. When we feel vulnerable, shyness draws a curtain between us, we hide behind it, just as we proclaim ourselves when we show off. She describes the characteristics of a shy response as those of blushing, bashful smiles or coy looks sideways and continues:

> When they are innocent reactions to the heightened visibility of the self to another person they can be charming…the charm of self-consciousness may lie precisely in this visibility of a previously hidden self – in seeing a self made ambivalent by the awareness of being laid bare by contact with another person. (Reddy 2006)

She gives as an example a specific interaction we all recognize as part of the lexicon of our behaviours where, in response to a suggestion that her conversation partner found slightly overwhelming, 'she half turned away with both body and face, although still with some positive affect, still smiling, and refusing to reveal what was asked' and suggests that it is 'specifically the visibility of self to others that is being managed here'.

I am pursuing Vasu's exploration because it is so insightful (and relevant when we return to autism).

> It is the ambivalent reactions of coyness, bashfulness and embarrassment which are usually seen as self-conscious because they seem to indicate a much more complex tension between affiliation and avoidance with an explicit acknowledgement of the self that is exposed.

However, if we then start to compare these reactions in children with and without autism, studies suggest that those children on the autistic spectrum, who are supposed to have difficulties in the perception of emotions in others, do not exhibit the features associated with shyness – the blushing, coyness, and so on – and by implication this reflects on the difficulties they are supposed to have with perception of self.

And here we hit a paradox. Careful examination of the Pranve tapes mentioned above shows that when we first meet Pranve (a man on the autistic spectrum with very severe behavioural distress) he displays his anxiety by sitting with his body slightly turned away from me. After a few minutes of using his sounds with him, he apparently decides that I am all right, half stands and turns, settling back in his chair so that we are now facing each other. Rolling his eyes he gives me a shy smile, lowers his chin and looks away *still smiling*, before turning his head back to look at me with a reassured full-on grin. It felt as if he was caught between conflicting emotions, a sort of pleasure that he could hardly bear and almost a flirtation with his own over-powerful affect, which finally came out in favour of interaction. It was the first growth-point in our relationship. It felt as if the introduction had been made and we could now get on with the business of getting to know and enjoy each other.

One of the triggers to an embarrassment-type reaction is described in Reddy's book as being triggered by the unexpected onset of meaningful attention, by mutual gaze and greeting. As in the Pranve exchange described above, although we had many other full-on smiles, it was only at the first 'self greeting self' meeting that this particular shyness reaction showed itself.

The point is here that the body language exchange described here between myself and Pranve is completely identical, it does not deviate in any respect, from that which is described for non-autistic persons. So what is the difference here between those children with autism who do not display such affective shyness and the situation where Pranve is clearly and demonstrably caught in the tangle of embarrassment and coy shyness?

We need to go back to the beginning of our encounter. As I wait at his front door, I am afraid of Pranve, not only because I have been warned that he may attack me, but also because of the familiar accompanying affect that can crudely be described as a fear of failure: I may be unable to get through to him, an emotion experienced in all such first meetings, particularly when my potential partners have a reputation for extremely disturbed behaviour. This nervousness reaches down deeply to touch who I think I am and what I think I am trying to do.

So anyway, here I am at the doorway, scared. His mother opens the door. Pranve is in another room. Before going in, before I invade his space, I listen to see if I can pick up any utterances he is making and yes, he is talking to himself with very soft little regular sounds, 'er-er-er', so I answer him, 'Er-er? er-er-er?', lifting my voice at the end in a question, in effect saying, 'Hello, can I come in?' I am introducing myself in a language which is significant and non-threatening for him. Immediately, this man who is so difficult and has a reputation for violent aggression, comes out and, taking my hand, leads me into the sitting room. I point to the sofa beside his chair and ask if I may sit. He points to the sofa – which

I take as 'yes' and sit down. The bashfulness incident takes place about five minutes after we have physically encountered each other, during which time we have been communicating with each other through his sounds and hand movements.

The difference lies in the *mode* of interaction. When I am 'talking' to Pranve, our dialogue is through body language rather than through speech. Using this form of communication he does not have to deal with and translate the confusion of what Donna Williams calls the 'Blah-Blah coming from out there', a sensory input which she describes as always involving an interpretation of the world of meaning. It is hardly surprising that if the brain is involved in a heroic struggle to make sense of what is going on in a world it experiences as one of terror, that it cannot simultaneously demonstrate an ability to reflect on the subtleties of the world of affect.

Communicating with Pranve through his preferred language cuts out the stress, so now his brain can begin to attend to its own processes. It is especially interesting that his capacity to make the switch does not take a long time, it is immediate, from a man whose brain is in a state of total chaos, always defensive, on red alert, attacking people to the point at which no one feels able to work with him, to a person who is lively and alert and charming, fun to be with and creative in the ways he communicates.

Pranve is not the only person with autism whose emotional responses to embarrassment have been recorded. Donna Williams herself shows an identical reaction in the 1993 documentary *My Experience with Autism, Emotion and Behavior* when asked whether she likes herself now she has found herself. Her chin goes down as she smiles and slightly turns away as she repeats the question (a delaying tactic), 'How do I like myself?' She turns back with an extremely shy smile and answers that yes, she thinks her 'self' is beautiful.

Despite any ideas we have about autism, Pranve and, in this case, Donna, were clearly touched. So I want to pause for a moment and consider what we mean when we talk about 'feeling touched' or 'feeling moved'.

First of all, there is nothing casual about this, this is touch-with-intent. If I say, 'I am touched', it is both present and retrospective – describing something you have done, consideration of which has awakened in me an internal sensation. It is an expression both of contact but also of the change this initiates in me. You have shown me – and I now see something different about myself.

If we want to understand what touch means in this sense we should look at Michelangelo's fresco of The Creation in the Sistine Chapel, where the great figure of God extends his forefinger to the perfect but as yet 'body-without-soul' Adam. Earlier frescos had depicted the two figures as separate, with the soul being passed over as a 'ray' or a 'psyche with butterfly wings' (Cronin 1969). The observer might know what is happening without feeling its power. What is missing is touch as transmission of feeling, a vehicle for affect. In Michelangelo's painting, God gives life and Adam accepts it through touch. Intimacy and tenderness crystallize. Man, Woman, Adam are changed, can never be the same.

Such an exchange involves offering, consideration, internalization and acceptance, and this is two-way. All the implications are that in a dyadic partnership both partners see something that they had not previously been aware of, and in so doing learn about themselves. In the heart of affect we are brought to the birthplace of consciousness.

All this is not to say that people with autism do not have a deficit in their ability to process facial language and what it means in terms of feelings. Under the normal – and for them chaotic – environment, they do find it hard, sometimes impossible, but if steps are taken to minimize stress, not only through the reduction of those inputs to which they are particularly sensitive but also by the use of their body language so that they can focus on something simple which does not require processing, the processes emerge intact. It is overload and the fear of fragmentation that makes it impossible for them to engage in affective dialogue. Once this is cleared out of the way, they are able to connect with themselves and others. The implication for practice is that all our energies should be directed to the reduction of stress.

In the next chapter we are going to look at 'Theory of Mind', a theory which attempts to explain how it is that people perceive, or fail to perceive what other people are thinking – and that they have a separate thought-life to their own.

6

Theory of Mind

The purpose of this chapter is to try and unravel current contradictions between theory and practice. I want to try and put the arguments as simply as possible.

In our search to penetrate the difficulties that people on the autistic spectrum are experiencing, two approaches have converged. Firstly, the Theory of Mind (Baron-Cohen *et al.* 1985) postulates that in order to relate to other people we need to be able to recognize and infer what other people are thinking. Secondly, what allows us to do this is our mirror neurones (specialized nerve cells which allow us to recognize what other people are doing) and these have been demonstrated to be dysfunctional in people with autism (Dapretto *et al.* 2006). Putting these together, if I am autistic, I cannot relate to you because my mirror neurones are not functioning normally.

In order for me to relate to you, I need to establish boundaries which tell me that you are not just an endless breast designed to fulfil my needs – but that you exist as a different entity. You are different from me and have different sensory perceptions and thoughts which may lead you to draw quite different conclusions from mine. And this is what (apparently) people on the autistic spectrum find so difficult that it makes it difficult or impossible for them to relate to others. It is this aloneness which is addressed by the Theory of Mind, and it is pivotal to understanding how we can move from isolation to friendship and even intimacy. It is like a hinge on the door of relationship. If it is in order (if I know you are different from me and can infer that you may have different thoughts), the door will swing open, at least potentially. If it is rusted, the door will remain shut; you are simply an extension of my expectations and there is no hope of true relatedness, of getting to know who you are or even being interested in this.

The consequences of applying Theory of Mind to autism are important in that they dominate current thinking and research. The evidence for doing so is considerable and supported by emerging neurobiological evidence. But in spite of this, I am going to suggest that such an application can be misleading, since its focus is on what people on the autistic spectrum cannot do, rather than on what they can do given optimum environmental conditions.

So, in the context of autism, what do we mean by Theory of Mind, a hypothesis which when applied to the popular image of people with autism sees them as remote and involved in repetitive behaviour? Meet Steven, a six-year-old boy on the autistic spectrum introduced in an article in the *New Scientist* by Vilayanur Ramachandran *et al.* (2006). Steven is described as unable to interact through normal two-way conversation, refuses to make eye-contact, fidgets and rocks to and fro. Attempts to communicate with him have failed, and his parents are despairing that they will ever be able to reach him.

This is the classical 'cut-offness' that is characteristic of autism. Many parents feel dispossessed of their child. They may have to endure a living bereavement to be grieved each day. Separation is not just spatial. Even when we are with them, children and adults on the spectrum may appear not to be present, disconnected, not at home. But it is important to realize that such isolation is not necessarily one-sided. One child described how it is for him: 'I feel like an alien in a foreign world.'

At first when I work with a child, I may not seem to have any significance to them as a human being. I am filled with a desire to know where they are and what is going on for them. Why am I so cut off as to feel like a lump of wood? If only I could look inside and see.

Now the window is beginning to open. Using new scanners, neurobiologists are starting to be able to link behaviours with simultaneous brain activity in ways that have not previously been possible. In particular, they are beginning to be able to make the link between activities in the nerve cells, neurones – which ones are firing at any particular time – and behaviours as they happen. What they are finding is that this neural network of mirror neurones is activated not only when we perform an action ourselves, but also when we see someone else perform the same activity (Astafiev *et al.* 2004). If you copy me, I know that it is me you are copying. In order for me to do this, I need to recognize what it is that you are doing.

Current research suggests that one of the reasons people on the autistic spectrum are having difficulties in reading the signs which indicate what another person is feeling – as opposed to what they themselves are feeling – is because their mirror neurones are not firing normally. In the words of Ramachandran *et al.* (2006):

> because people with autism have such profound deficits in social interaction, they lack the specialised brain mechanisms proposed by Frith and Baron-Cohen (1985) that create internal working models of the inner workings of other minds so they can predict the behaviours of others and manipulate them if need be.

The next step has been to see if the mirror neurones of an autistic child behave differently to those of a neurotypical child. This has been made possible by looking at the different components of an electro-encephalogram (EEG). What it shows is that in a neurotypical brain, the part of the EEG known as the 'mu wave' is blocked, not only if we make a movement but also when we see another person make the same gesture. So it has become possible to measure the activity of the mirror neurone system by measuring mu wave suppression. To put it simply, if our mirror neurones are working, the mu wave will be suppressed when we make an action, *or* when we recognize our action made by someone else. If we do not recognize our action made by someone else, the mu wave will fire intact.

Ramachandran looked at mu wave suppression in ten high-functioning children with autism and ten non-autistic controls. As expected, in children without autism, results showed a suppression of mu wave, both when they moved their hands and also when they watched video of hand movements. However, those children on the autistic spectrum showed mu suppression when they moved their own hands but not when they watched others move their hands (Ramachandran *et al.* 2006).

But (as discussed in *Finding You Finding Me*), here we have the discrepancy between what happens when you engage a person on the spectrum through their body language and the result obtained in research laboratories. If we approach this as anthropologists, observing what actually happens in real time rather than under experimental conditions, we notice that (although the characteristics highlighted in Steven earlier in this chapter are those we normally associate with children with autism), if we use communicative elements that are already part of a person's reper-toire to set up non-verbal conversation, people on the spectrum are very able to recognize, be interested in and engage with the body language of others. Under conditions which their brain perceives as tranquil, even those whose autism is allied to severe learning disability, distressed and sometimes violent behaviour can read and respond to what other people are feeling. Face muscles and body language relax. The eyes become alert and lively and interested in what is going on around them. They look round calmly and often show the desire for relationship, indeed are hungry for such engagement. Distressed and disturbed behaviour patterns alter. (For example, a week after the commencement of introduc-ing the use of his sounds to him – and so lowering his stress level by giving his brain something significant to relate to – a child who is self-injuring to the point of severe bruising has ceased to hit himself. His care team report that he no longer needs to be restrained but can be 'talked down'. His mother tells me that she has just had two wonderful evenings with him using his sounds.)

Admittedly, under the sensory conditions which are provided by his ordinary everyday environment, he is not able to engage. But it seems that we are being misled into conclusions about the potential capacity of a process by the bizarre behaviours that are the self-protective response to sensory overload, in the case of the child above, probably at least in part a reaction to severe hypersensitivity to light.

The work that I and many other practitioners who use body language to engage our partners have done with people with severe autism (and which they and I have described at length in the literature) demonstrates repeatedly that if the interaction is taking place under what we experi-ence as normal conditions (but for the autistic person may be a state of total sensory confusion), in order to obtain a response the action to which they are responding must already be part of their existing significant rep-ertoire. *The act must be something their brain already recognizes as familiar* (a situation that recalls the work mentioned in Chapter 4 on the capacity of neurotypical infants to predict an event once they had already learned it: Falck-Ytter *et al.* 2006). This point is entirely overlooked by the main-stream psychological research literature – and it is this absence that produces the conflict of evidence between what researchers claim that people on the spectrum cannot do – and what use of body language demonstrates they actually can do if sensory conditions they experience as calm prevail.

There is a further problem with the literature. Having concluded that people on the spectrum are incapable of responding to others, researchers have to explain the cause of this 'failure'. Theory of Mind argues that there is a deficit in their cognitive capacities. That is, they do not have the cognitive skills to pay attention to and to interpret other people's facial expressions and to draw conclusions about their internal mental states and feelings. Indeed they are not even interested in these (Baron-Cohen *et al.* 1985). This account is now the most influential explanation as to why people on the spectrum are so poor at social engagement – and it guides much research funding and therapeutic work.

However, this theory is based on the critical assumption that people with autism and learning disabilities lack the capacity to engage and socialize. The researchers have sought to explain why this 'failure' exists. But the idea that there is such an underlying failure is completely contrary to the findings and experience of practitioners of Intensive Interaction, who are quite often being asked to work with people that are seen as highly disturbed and sometimes dangerous, and with whom it is proving difficult to find staff willing to engage. Nevertheless, if we use their body language with such people, even they are able to respond and socialize *if we interact with them in a language that has significance for their brain.* Essentially I am suggesting that the application of Theory of Mind to autism is based on a false premise. It is not that people on the spectrum are incapable of communication and relationship because of deficient cognitive capacities or even incorrectly firing mirror neurones. When we use the body language based on an individual's personal repertoire we find that they are able to engage – but that this is only apparent when the 'vocabulary' that is being used is one that already has meaning for the brain. Very simply, if we wish to talk with them, we must do so in a language they understand.

For people with autism it is stress that is the problem. The more stressed they are the less easy it is to process. The question is why are they so stressed?

A recent comparison of skin conductance in children with autism with those not on the spectrum shows a high level of autonomic arousal in children on the spectrum as opposed to neurotypical children (Ramachandran 2006). (Skin conductance is a measure of sweating and this indicates activity in the autonomic nervous system.) This is in accord with personal, long-term observations of people with autism during episodes of loss of coherence and fragmentation, such as excessive sweating – to the point where sweat occasionally comes out in fountains that clear right off the skin rather than in trickles or beads – and capillary dilation. A possible further clue is that oxytocin, a hormone implicated in the control of the autonomic nervous system, has been found to reduce repetitive behaviours (Hollander *et al.* 2003). Finally, however they are triggered, the personal descriptions of the neurobiological sensations experienced by people such as Gunilla Gerland and Donna Williams also point towards distortions in the autonomic nervous system: the fizziness and pains in the nape of the neck and spine that branch out throughout the body during what Ramachandran suggests should be thought of as 'autonomic storms'.

In the same article Ramachandran also goes on to say that, rather than being non-functional, the mirror neurones may be dormant in people with autism and that there may be conditions under which they could be activated. We believe that such conditions apply when we use an individual's own body language and that this accounts for the increased effectiveness of brain function as demonstrated by their increasing ability to relate, to generalize, and so on. To argue that I cannot relate because my brain lacks the capacity to do so is like saying I cannot add up in Mongolian, whereas my difficulty lies in my inability to recognize the symbols as numbers.

In an investigation on imitation and identification in people with autism, Hobson and Lee (1999) introduce a variety of tasks to children with autism with the aim of seeing whether the child can imitate the 'style' in which the task is carried out – as opposed to the ability to carry out the task itself. Their results highlight the difficulties that those on the spectrum experience in picking up the affective content of a communication. This is hardly surprising, since an analysis of the scan-paths of faces showing emotion, particularly of fear, suggests that the eyes of people on the spectrum avoid those parts of the face which are indicators of affect (Pelphrey *et al.* 2002). As a mother told me her son with autism said: 'I've learned to look at the chin rather than the eyes because looking at the eyes hurts.' So it is difficult to pick up what people are feeling if you are avoiding this facial element of language.

However, Smith and Bryson (1994) point out that the difficulties people on the spectrum have with imitating others may be connected with language processing difficulties rather than with capacity to copy as such. Hobson and Lee (1999) also quote Sigman and Ungerer (1984): 'Insofar as individuals with autism have difficulty in perceiving and/or executing novel movements or movement sequences, this may need to be distinguished from the ability to copy goal-directed actions'.

When psychologists design experiments that rely on visual contact and focus on the spoken language, they are actually using elements of communication that the individual may find threatening: the principal threat being that overloading the sensory system may tip them into the painful feedback known as fragmentation, the 'autonomic storm' proposed by Ramachandran. Thus current research leads us to draw conclusions about the 'absence' of a process which, when the brain is unstressed, can be seen to be functioning normally (within the cognitive capacity of the individual). Coincident with relaxation in body and facial language, there is a decrease in repetitive behaviour and distressed and challenging behaviour, an increase in eye-contact, and an increase in engagement with their surroundings and emotional engagement (Zeedyk and Caldwell 2006). Such details as the ability to generalize emerge intact, just as is the case for neurotypical people. Depending on the level of learning disability, speech may appear in non-verbal people and become more relevant in those who have some speech. With its combination of sensory overload and fear of fragmentation, people with autism are living on the front line of an affective battle zone. I suggest that it is this, rather than cognitive and neuronal deficits, that is leading to processing difficulties and all the difficulties in comprehension and relationship that follow from these.

As mentioned above, Pranve, who is diagnosed by his consultant psychiatrist as having severe autism, is extremely hypersensitive to high frequency sound and is constantly attacking the people round him to the extent that it has become difficult to provide a service for him. During a four-hour session throughout which I am using his sounds and movements to communicate with him, he becomes so relaxed that he no longer takes notice of the planes with their high-pitched whine that are coming in to land so low over the rooftop that it feels as if their wheels are scraping the ridge of his roof. When it is time to go, he has left us and is sitting quietly in the front room. I do not want to invade his space, so I say goodbye to him from the passage – but when I am outside the front door, something special seems to be called for. Pranve is sitting near the window, so I splay out my hand and place it on the outer side of the glass. Far from being unable to identify and respond to my gesture, Pranve glances down at his own hand which is lying loosely curled on his lap, carefully unrolls it and slowly spreading out his fingers, places his hand on the other side of the glass to match mine. Just to spell out the implications of such a response, in order for him to recognize and copy such a hand movement, presumably his mu waves must have been suppressed in the same way that a neurotypical person's would have been. Since he is autistic, this is precisely the hand gesture that the mu wave experimental evidence has suggested that he should not be able to copy. In this case, his mirror neurones were responding in the same way as those of a person who is not on the spectrum.

How can we explain this? I would suggest that, just because under 'normal' conditions the mirror neurones are not firing does not necessarily mean they are unable to do so. To use an analogy, under the chaotic conditions which are normal for the brain of a person with autism, it is like saying we are unable to start a car when the engine is flooded. This does not mean the motor is incapable of working, but rather that our practice is at fault. When Pranve's brain is relaxed, far from being unable to copy what I do, the way that he meets and imitates my novel and unexpected gesture is quite deliberate and thought out. It is also extremely moving.

For another example, I want to move ahead to Chapter 13, where there is a discussion of interventions used with a small child, Harriet, who has very severe autism and, particularly, sensory hypersensitivities that make it extremely difficult for her to interact. Her occupational therapist has been using proprioceptive stimulation (Sensory Integration) with her, combining this with using her body language, which she says has made it easier for her to interact with her. Now that Harriet is relaxed, she speeds up and slows down her babbling according to the tempo of the exercise that her therapist is using. The rhythm is something her brain can process without fear of overload – but her imitation is cross-modal. Once again, she is demonstrating capacities that Theory of Mind suggests she should not possess.

These two stories are particularly interesting because although we have discussed the delight that people on the autistic spectrum have when their partners use imitation with them, we have hardly touched on the particular difficulties they exhibit in deficits in ability to imitate others. I want to say again that, in my view, it is the degree to which an individual can relax from the turmoil in their brains that determines whether or not they can comprehend and relate. It is not a question of their ultimate capacity to do so.

Donna Williams, although she speaks four languages, describes for us the extraordinary effect that hearing one of her own sounds has on her – 'like being thrown a lifebelt in a stormy sea' – literally life saving.

In fact, once we have established a way of communicating, most partners will not waste time on imitation – but will almost immediately go on to introduce new material, referring back and testing me out to see what we shall make of it. They want real communication (in my experience, are desperate for it and demonstrate this by their urgent desire for physical contact) but find it difficult to make connection with the type of assignments that characterize contemporary research protocols, since they are conducted in a 'language' that the brain does not recognize.

What sort of body language are we looking for to tell us that our non-verbal partner wants to know what we are thinking? Lucy is very withdrawn and beats her cheek so badly that the bone is exposed. It takes twenty minutes before she realizes that each time she hits herself, I respond by tapping my own cheek. As described in *You Don't Know What It's Like*, when she realizes that she is receiving a contingent response, her jaw drops in surprise. She starts to smile and then embarks on a whole programme of movements which are new to the staff who are looking after her, stretching her arms up and out and always referring back to me to see what I will make of it. Every time I get it right, she laughs but appears disappointed if I do not respond correctly. In effect she is interested in what I think about what she is doing, it matters to her.

Recently I spent a week working with twelve people who in one form or another were withdrawn into and lost in their own inner worlds. None had I met before and none had so far responded in any way to the variety of approaches used by the teams of professionals and support staff working with them. In most cases, the reason I had been asked to see if I could get in touch with them was that they were severely behaviourally disturbed and all attempts to make contact with them were failing. One spent his life looking at his hand movements, another was locked into a computer game in an alcove. A third had shut himself away in a darkened room. If these and other patterns of behaviour were interrupted, they became upset and aggressive. As soon as I began to use their own body language with them, they recognized 'their initiatives coming from outside themselves', abandoned their self-stimulatory activities and came and joined me wherever I was, giving good eye-contact and laughing and joining in. All twelve responded with interest and pleasure as soon as I used their sounds or movements. I was able to show their support staff how to use this technique with them before I left.

Once we have developed a meaningful common mode of interaction, we find that even in the most withdrawn people on the autistic spectrum, the desire and ability to communicate are intact. This contrasts strongly with what is predicted by Theory of Mind and suggests that 'we can only form theories of mind if we take into account states of mind' (Nicholas Colloff, personal communication).

Just to summarize, circumstances which are normal for neurotypicals are processed by people with severe autistic spectrum disorder as intimidating, hostile, confusing and sometimes painful. Most of them are not able to look at people, socialize, generalize, understand speech or use it, and yet these same people can do, and willingly do, these things in conditions which they experience as calm and non-threatening. In these situations, their so-called challenging behaviour is diminished and often extinguished. They understand a lot more speech and may learn to use it relevantly. The barriers to eye-contact are lowered, and they increasingly seek out meaningful contact by direct gaze. Their desire and capacity to interact is evidenced not just by increased physical contact but quite often also by what can only be described as joy.

Anyone who is suggesting that a person on the autistic spectrum is never able to understand the emotional experience of another person should read Kamran Nazeer's (also on the spectrum) powerful and yet sensitive analysis of the ins and outs of the relationship between Randall and Mike in his book *Send in the Idiots* (2006).

Why does this matter so much? What is at stake is the practice that is developed from theory. We now have a way of helping people with autism – and those with severe learning disability – to live lives in which they feel comfortable, in which they can relate, and through which they can use such cognitive capacity that they possess unchecked by confusion, fear and sensory overload. We should be bending all our intelligence to this purpose.

7

How Well Does Using a Person's Body Language Work?

Personal Practice

Since no two people are the same, the particular way that we use body language to develop relationship is inevitably intensely personal and no partnership will grow in exactly the same way as another so at this point I need to explain something about how it is that I work. This usually involves being asked to see people whose situation is judged to be in crisis. As a general rule, I see them in the morning, if possible video our work (together with their support partner) and teach the staff team in the afternoon. Even during this short period, it is normal for there to be effective change. On the whole I do not need to return, although the staff team are encouraged to get back to me if they are in doubt. It should be said that since the situation is normally judged to be critical, staff are usually motivated to continue the work once they can see some way out of the difficulties with which they are struggling. This means, however, that most of the accounts I can offer are cross-sections, 'a day in the life of...' accounts. The condition of permanent change is that staff continue to develop and use their interactive skills. As described in my earlier books (Caldwell with Hoghton 2000; Caldwell 2002a, 2006a), and particularly in the case of people on the autistic spectrum, if the interactions are withdrawn (as has happened on one or two occasions when a new team leader has decided that the person is now 'better') regression is instant. On the other hand, provided the interactions are maintained, improvement both in behaviour and general desire to relate is open-ended and sometimes astonishing. People who have been in great distress can live happily, and the effect is also to be seen in those who care for them. But I should emphasize that this end is achieved by sustained practice and an environment that upholds this. To break off is as if, having taught a child to speak, we decide we have done what is necessary and no longer talk to them.

A young man who was working with a partner whose behaviour made it difficult to be with him, since he was so aggressive, admitted that before he learned to use his partner's body language, he had been anxious every day about coming to work but was now able to relax. Now, they are able to have a really good time together: 'Just generally, our life is much more relaxed, much better.'

But first of all, as an introduction to work with people with severe and multiple disability not on the autistic spectrum, I want to introduce three people with cerebral palsy, Lynne, Gemma and Hannah.

In the training video *Creative Conversations* Lynne, who is in her late twenties, has very severe cerebral palsy and epilepsy (Caldwell and Stevens 2005). She lies in a chair and has little movement except in her head. The manager of the day centre she attends says that staff are very concerned for her as they have no way of communicating with her and the only sounds she makes are those of distress. When we visit her, she is initially silent and motionless so there appears to be no body language to respond to. So I ask her support partner to try 'kick-starting' a conversation by using one of the sounds she is known to make – and therefore one she is likely to recognize. After an initial absence, Lynne begins to answer our sounds, at first making very small ones. As her confidence grows, these become louder and are accompanied by smiling and eventually laughing. On the video her body language is of a person gathering strength as she puts more and more effort into her responses. Finally, her manager says she has never seen her laugh before.

For those of us who took part in this coming together it was, as it normally is, an intensely moving experience. This particular interaction is especially interesting in that it was we who initiated the conversation by using elements of her language which we had learned from her support partner, expressive sounds which had not previously been thought to have communicative potential. Introducing these sounds that Lynne recognized as familiar, shifted her attention from her inner world to their source outside herself.

In the same video we meet Gemma whose family have been using Intensive Interaction with her for about six months. Gemma is severely disabled, sits in a wheelchair and is tube-fed. Her adoptive sister who is her main carer describes the difference it has made to them all since they learned to use her sounds and movements and how it has changed the quality of her life. She can now express how she feels because people are more responsive to her body language. 'She has become more communicative in many ways, more demanding but in a wholly beneficial way. Life is better for Gemma.'

Finally in this group of non-ambulant people with cerebral palsy I want to introduce Hannah, who was previously described in *Person to Person* (Caldwell and Stevens 1998). I do so because her story is less straightforward than those of Lynne and Gemma. In addition to using Intensive Interaction her timetable needed to be restructured in small but significant ways.

I meet Hannah in a day centre. Fully grown, she lies in her wheelchair and is very small indeed. She has no sight at all. I am asked to see her because her behaviour is causing problems at the day centre in that she screams loudly at dinner, when she is in the hoist and when she is about to travel on the coach. The screaming at dinner is a particular problem as it upsets other students and sets off a chain reaction of chaotic noise. So far, unsuccessful attempts to modify her behaviour have focused on helping her to learn to wait for it to be served. An alternative approach is to try and see how her day looks to her.

Some people with cerebral palsy seem to be very hungry. In Hannah's case, food is the most important thing in her life. Hannah is only really happy when her stomach is full. When she reaches the dining room she can smell the food but because she is blind, she cannot see the preparations for its arrival. Often there is a long wait, ten to fifteen minutes. She becomes increasingly distressed. By the time she is served, she is screaming loudly. She is fed by spoon and eats fast – then there is another ten-minute wait before her sweet arrives, which she particularly enjoys as she has a sweet tooth. So she screams again. This is communication. She is telling us what she wants.

Once we look at the situation from the point of view of a person who is blind and hungry and unable to know that her meal is on the way, we can take effective action by making sure that she is never brought to the dining area until her food is ready and that there is no delay between the first and second course. Instead of trying to control her, we are listening to her needs as expressed through her body language.

Hannah also screams when she is lifted, either manually or in the hoist. A look of sheer terror came over her face when she was lifted, even though the staff who lifted her were careful and very gentle. Her reaction suggested pain and the fear of pain. The latter can be just as upsetting as pain itself – a blueprint in the mind which, as a result of some past incident, is painful enough to cause spasm when she is being lifted. (Fear is just as potent if it is apprehensive rather than contingent.)

At this stage I started to listen more carefully to her body language and noticed that when she was eating (an activity which is the highlight of her day and is associated with pleasure) her jaw made a curious clicking sound.

For Hannah, these sounds are an integral part of her most positive internal sensation, eating, and she is fascinated when I use them as a way of talking to her during periods when she is normally afraid, for example before getting on the hoist at the back of the coach and when she is being lifted. Interest in her 'happy sounds' overrides her fear of being lifted by relocating her attention. She is quiet during the period of departure, a time when she usually screams.

The spectrum of Hannah's feelings are expressed in body language through screams for anxiety and fear and through click sounds associated with pleasurable activity. By listening to her, we can modify those parts of her daily life which raise her stress level and calm her when she is afraid.

Had Hannah been deaf as well as blind it would have been more difficult to answer her clicks, but in similar circumstances I have been successful through using a tap instead of a sound to respond, or a bounce or vibration where my partner can feel my answer. Not surprisingly, the individual is delighted as soon as they realize there is a world out there they can connect with.

Moving on now to the even more difficult field of communication with people who are blind-deaf, an interesting paper by Paul Hart, the Principal Officer for Practice Development, SENSE, Scotland, traces the movement from the idea of teaching the less-skilled person 'our language' towards equality in communication partners where the contributions of both partners are valued (Hart 2003). Vonen and Nafstad (1999) point out that all naturally developed languages are dependent on vision or hearing and there has never been a natural tactile language. Yet, of necessity, this is the only way that people who are deaf-blind can access communication, which in this case is defined as sharing understanding.

Deaf-blindness should not be thought of as a negative state but one in which touch is the primary vehicle for communication. The child has to be seen as co-contributor to interaction. Rødbroe and Souriau (2000) are critical of the idea that communication is simply a messaging system and point to the need for sustained and joyful communication episodes. The skilled partner should follow the child's lead so as to create a new negotiated way of communication.

Validation

Inevitably we need proof. How do we know if it works? The practitioner would say that the quickest way to find out if it works is to go and try it. Those who have been using it for many years know that as an approach it is extremely successful and the time it takes to effect behavioural change can be very quick. No elaborate programmes, just using what psychologists loosely call 'imitation', valuing all that a person is doing as having meaning – and even if they are on the autistic spectrum the child or adult partner will normally recognize this and respond. The outcomes are relaxation, increased sociability and a decrease in distressed behaviour.

One of the problems with convincing psychologists that the use of body language in the way we have been describing (the approach known as Intensive Interaction) is effective, is that until recently much of the evidence has been in the form of anecdotal single-case studies. In this chapter we need to look at the increasing evidence that use of imitation and body language increases the desire to engage and relate.

For example, by using frame-by-frame analyses of video material it is possible to code the growth of interpersonal engagement in terms of four variables – eye gaze, proximity to the partner and positive emotion. In a paper currently in preparation, Zeedyk and Caldwell (2006) are able to demonstrate clearly that Intensive Interaction, in the form of responsive initiation, promotes social engagement. However broken down, study after study shows the same pattern – that although the time taken to effect change may differ (in some cases the time-line is short, in others longer) the sequence is the same: imitation is accompanied by an increase in intimacy.

Turning now to clinical studies in other branches of learning disability, Barber (2006) points out that one of the major difficulties facing the process of setting up clinical trials into Intensive Interaction is the immense variety of disabilities with which it is useful and is used. There are ongoing research projects both in the educational field and in the field of child development.

At Bayside Special Development School in Moorabbin, Australia, Mark Barber has been running a project using Intensive Interaction with children on the autistic spectrum with behavioural and communication difficulties. Up to fifteen children, ranging in age from five to sixteen, are involved in the Moorabbin pilot project. None have any formal communication skills. 'All but one has been diagnosed as being on the autistic spectrum. These are young people who have tended to be very hard to reach. They may have a very solitary focus, not willing at all to communicate with the outside world' (Barber 2006). A preliminary report awaiting publication suggests that the Principal and staff are delighted with their progress. For example, the most difficult child is now calmer, starting to use words and beginning to enjoy interaction with others instead of living in a world of screaming and tantrums.

In the field of child development, there are now many studies which point in one direction, that using imitation increases sociability, even if the partner is on the autistic spectrum. Bearing in mind what we have said about the relationship of imitation to Intensive Interaction, what follows is a look at some of the current literature on the use of imitation.

In a study of spontaneous imitation in the play of a mixed group of eight children with developmental delay (one with Down's syndrome and two with visual disability) and their carers, O'Neill and Zeedyk (2006) showed that when the adults imitated the children, although they did not respond with imitative actions, there was a significant increase in subsequent social behaviours, such as smiles and speech vocalizations, indicating awareness of having been imitated.

In studies of children with autism, Nadel et al. (2000) have used the approach known as 'still face', an interaction between autistic child and adult which takes its name from sessions where the adult is unresponsive to what the child does, sitting like a statue for sessions of three minutes. They record the number of social behaviours in a series of three-minute sessions (looking at the person, positive and negative expressions, social gestures, close proximity and touching.) Four sessions follow each other:

1.   'still face'

2.   'imitation of child by adult'

3.   'still face'

4.   'spontaneous interaction'.

In session 1, the child ignored the still adult – but in session 3, after a period where the adult imitated the child, there were significantly more expectant behaviours than were recorded in session 1. These included coming to the adult and touching them as if to induce the interactive behaviour of the previous session. In this and similar work by Escalona *et al.* (2000) periods of imitation are followed by increased interaction as compared with those before an imitation session. In the latter case the authors suggest that an increase in negative facial expressions reflects disappointed expectation that they are no longer receiving a response.

In a study of twenty children with autism, Field *et al.* (2001) show that increased sessions of imitation of children by adults are followed by an increase in behaviours such as looking, smiling and vocalizing at the adult, and reciprocal play, indicating the child's desire to be close to the adult.

In Norway, in a comparative study of the effects of specifically imitative play as against contingent play, using the still-face procedure with children with autism as described above, Heimann, Laberg and Nordøen (2006) showed there was a significant increase in the frequency of social interactions following imitative play but not after contingent play.

Returning to individual studies, this desire to be close and to explore a dawning relationship is extremely powerfully illustrated in the training video *Learning the Language*, where Gabriel, a man with very severe autism and learning disability who has not previously demonstrated any ability to interact socially, peers deeply into the eyes of his partner, smiling at her, initiating a new behaviour and offering this back to her to see what she will make of it. His close exploration of her face is almost painful to watch (Caldwell 2002b).

From these studies and a considerable number of others (e.g. Dawson and Adams 1984, Dawson and Galpert 1990) it is clear that imitation, which forms the bases of Intensive Interaction, facilitates an increase in social interaction.

In practice, a mother tells me that she thought she knew her son (who has speech) until she tried using the sounds he also made. She says that she had not realized how important these sounds were to him. Responding to them had opened up new aspects of his personality and she understood him much better. And a psychiatrist recently put the case for Intensive Interaction when he said: 'Up until now we have run out of options. This approach offers hope for the people for whom we had nothing to offer.'

What else do we need to do apart from using body language?

We have seen already how effective it is in reaching deep into our partner's feeling world and altering the way they can respond and relate. While it is clear that Intensive Interaction is not a cure, it is clearly more than just a good sticking plaster. For example with Hannah, although we were able to divert her attention away from her fear of being lifted by using clicks which she recognized as part of her repertoire, we also needed to restructure her timetable, so that she was not subjected to long delays during which period she could hear and smell preparations for lunch but because she had no sight, could not see that no one else was getting theirs, so she thought she was being left out.

And Ron, who we met previously, was sitting in a wheelchair even though he can walk. This is because, buried in the sensory chaos that is his life experience, the one feedback that has meaning for him is the proprioceptive sensation he receives from sitting in the chair – one might say he feels balanced and grounded by this. Without it he is in sensory freefall so it would be virtually impossible for him to attend even to his recognizable sounds.

So what limits are their on Intensive Interaction? If it works so easily, reaching as it does into the centre of our partner's affective world, how often does it stand on its own? Or is it always part of an approach which seeks to understand *why* our partner is upset? The following chapters look at Intensive Interaction in context, to see if we can define its parameters. Are there other times when we also need to modify the environment or change our practice in order to improve the quality of people's lives?

Chapter 8 looks at three children on the autistic spectrum who exemplify the three predominantly different ways of trying to reduce sensory overload, through focus on repetitive behaviour, through withdrawal and through aggression.

Part 2

Meeting People

8

Three Children on the Autistic Spectrum

Non-verbal people speak to us through their body language. In order to interpret what they are saying to us we need, as Donna Williams put it, to become anthropologists, sticking our own reality in our back pockets and teasing out the meaning of individual behaviours. This means investing our partner's gestures and utterances with meaning that, on the basis of our own experience of reality, we might overlook. Apart from their gender and the fact that the three children featured in this chapter have autism, they really have nothing in common. As we immerse ourselves in their world, their individual personalities become more and more evident and each presents as a completely different individual with their own particular flavour. We see the same view but with different eyes.

But first, before we meet Davy, Niall and Alex, a teacher tells me about another small boy who, instead of playing with other children or on the equipment at break, patrols the perimeter fence, round and round, round and round. His teacher says he is difficult to make contact with – but one day she says to him, 'Can I do it too?'

To her surprise he answers her, 'Yes, it's my favourite thing this.'

He cannot tell her why – but she plods round with him. She says that since then, they seem to have had a special bond.

According to a speaker in the 1992 Channel 4 film *A is for Autism*, break times at school were a particular problem for another boy when he was a child. The text of this film is especially revealing.

> At nursery school on bright days my sight blurred. sometimes when the others spoke to me I could scarcely hear them – their

voices sounded like bullets and I thought I was going to go deaf. The other kids would not let me join in their games even when I wanted to. They thought I was mad because I was all tensed up and had a way of flapping my hands and I came across as being different and other kids don't like kids who are different.

A playground is by definition an area of disorganized activity. In the film we see children running in every direction, the child is surrounded by unpredictable movements and waves of sound. His vision and hearing have collapsed. He doesn't know what is happening, it is too much for his brain to process. So he takes refuge in a repetitive behaviour, flapping his hands – or, as in the case of the first child, patrolling the playground fence. At least when these children do these activities, they know what they are doing. (Sometimes people refer to such activities as 'comfort activities' but this is to underestimate the threat of over-stimulation, which can so easily tip into catastrophic fragmentation with its associated pain and confusion.) Better by far to funnel all attention into a pattern with which the brain is familiar so as to exclude the world outside.

In Chapter 3 we looked at the coping strategies developed by children and some adults on the autistic spectrum, which enable them to cut down on overloading input. The first is to focus on a repetitive sensation or behaviour, as the two children we have just met are doing and as does Davy (who has a fixation on words he sees on TV which he then reproduces in play-dough) who we shall meet in this chapter. Secondly, a child can withdraw from the situation. Niall simply opts out, hiding in his room, squeezed under the far corner of his bed with a blanket round him and a pillow over his head. Alternatively, like Alex, the child can become aggressive, trying to get rid of the source (as they rightly or wrongly perceive it) of the overloading sensory experience.

Davy

Davy is a small boy with severe ASD. As he walks down the passage he trails his fingers along the woodchip wallpaper. (This is a sensation so familiar that I do not have to do it in order to feel what he is feeling. It is recorded in my flesh and I can play back the track of its sensation and recoil simply by thinking about it.)

First of all, it would be wrong to dismiss this as just something he does. We need to try and put ourselves into his position in order to see why he does it. In his chaotic sensory perception of his environment the roughness of the paper is a tactile sensation he is using to orientate himself, so he knows where he is in relation to the wall. This sensation is hard-wired in, it is one that his body understands. It does not trigger processing overload. Other people I have known will orientate themselves similarly by kicking, sniffing or licking the walls. All are engaged in the practice of trying to make sense of their environment, using an alternative sensory mode when their visual sense threatens to overload.

Davy is eight. He has been at his present school for seven months. By providing a structured environment his teachers have already made great progress in reducing his outbursts and screaming, which went on all the time when he first arrived. His distress is now sporadic rather than continuous. However, he is still totally locked into his own world. Even when he is using his Picture Exchange Communication System (PECS) to let people know his choice of activity, he normally does this in such a way as to avoid personal interaction – it appears to simply be a way he has learned to deal with the world outside and get what he wants. There is no eye-contact, no spark in his face. The simplest way to describe him is that he is 'switched off', compliant but not engaged in the process in a way that indicates the desire for personal contact.

In saying this, I don't wish to undervalue the importance of a structured routine and the use of symbols. In Davy's case, even if his PECS symbols are not directly leading him to personal interaction, they do give him a stability, he knows what he is doing and can choose what he wants, and this is critical for him. But the difficulty remains that while he becomes competent in extracting what he wants from the world outside he learns to do this without ever crossing over and engaging with it in any personal sense. In order to obtain such a transfer, we need to look elsewhere. Is there a way of enhancing social skills as well as focusing on the teaching of cognitive skills?

When we try working with Davy, answering his sounds, he does not appear to connect with these either. However, Davy is the little boy who we first met in Chapter 3 when I described how he was totally absorbed in the novel sensation provided by gently pushing his swing sideways, a new direction for him. His interest in touch (the sensation generated in his fingers by the rough wall) and movement, suggests that the key to understanding how to get through to Davy is to take seriously his interest in vestibular, tactile and proprioceptive sensations. This insight was re-inforced by his behaviour on the see-saw.

Davy likes to rock on this piece of equipment with his teacher. I put the sounds he makes to himself together with his movement, emphasiz-ing the jerk as he rocks back and forth (two elements of his language in unfamiliar juxtaposition). He begins to smile, turning round and looking at each of us, searching out our faces in turn to see if we were enjoying his pleasure. What had been a solitary activity has become a social one. This lasts for two or three minutes – and then he is off again into his private world. Nevertheless, we have met him in a new way, one that leaves an imprint of his personality, how he feels. For me, it feels as if our relation-ship has moved from a two-dimensional one to three- dimensions.

Before Davy goes out, he needs to be changed into a weatherproof jacket and trousers. When he is dressed he sits on the stool with his feet on a chair, rocking back and forth. Now his teacher uses his sounds, attach-ing them to the rhythm of his movements. His face has relaxed and he is smiling at her.

One of the problems that his staff encounter is that on the way from one place to another, Davy will lie down and refuse to go on in spite of having seen a visual clue as to where he is supposed to be going. However, we decide to try and see what happens and if there is any way round his behaviour.

On the way inside from his playtime, Davy lies down as usual on the fire escape and clings to the metal framework. Previously the procedure at this point has been for his two support workers to lift him up and escort him inside. In fact he had responded to this so badly, screaming and becoming distraught, that his time outside had been severely restricted. So we need to try and understand what this lying down is about.

Gunilla Gerland was hypersensitive to the sound of motorbikes. She tells us that when they realized this the boys used to tease her, waiting un-til she had passed and then suddenly revving up. When she began to lose coherence in her mind, she had to cling on to a fence.

> Up and down were suddenly in the same place and I had no idea where my feet were. So as not to fall over or explode from inside, I had to grab the fence where I was standing, pressing myself against it and holding on hard. I had to feel something that stood still, something anchored in a world that had become totally un-predictable. (Gerland 1996)

Like Gunilla, when Davy feels he is losing track of his senses, he sensibly lies down and holds on, in this case to the ornamental ironwork.

I suggest we let Davy lie. Every time he makes a sound, I nudge his foot with mine. He is getting a tactile response to each of his sounds. After a short while he kneels up and pushes his fingers through the mesh. I meet his fingers with mine from the other side and tickle them each time he makes a sound. He pushes his nose against the mesh. This time I stroke his nose each time he vocalizes. He splays his hands on the grid. Taking my pen, I run it round his hands so that it makes the sound of metallic vibration. He keeps moving his fingers for me to do it again. Then he quite suddenly gets up and walks in unassisted.

What has happened here? I am working on the assumption that when Davy refuses to go on and lies down he has lost track of what is happening – and like Gunilla he has to find an anchor – something to hang on to in a sensory world which has ceased to make sense. For Davy, the most likely way to be able to re-establish contact is through his sense of touch, since this appears to be how he orientates himself, keeps in touch with reality. So I use tactile messages, banging his foot, etc. (even drawing my pen across the metal grid on which his hand is resting to make it vibrate). I want to re-anchor him in my world in a way that is safe, by offering him stimuli which do not add to his confusion. This shift of focus proves to be enough to get him going again.

Bearing in mind his affinity for tactile and proprioceptive clues, the next day when we want him to come in, I suggest that rather than using a picture as prompt (which had been proving ineffective in that although it started him off in the right direction, it was not a sufficiently strong clue to carry him through the task of getting inside), we used his play-dough pot as a clue with plenty of dough inside to give it weight and get him to carry it in, so offering him a persistent rather than a transitory reminder. This time he walked straight inside without stopping.

Davy has an unusual fixation which involves watching TV – and then writing out the words he sees, for example, 'WALT DISNEY', fashioning the letters with great precision out of play-dough. No matter how unusual or elaborate the font, he reproduces exactly what he has seen. When he has assembled his text he contemplates it with total attention before scrunching the letters up and repeating the exercise.

So far, Davy has been unwilling to allow others to join his letter fixation activity but his teachers have sat beside him and used another colour. I decided to try and get a bit closer. When I took bits off his lump of play-dough, at first he snatched them back but after a little while grew more tolerant of my interventions, especially when I deliberately made the wrong letter and added them to the word the he was making, this was funny and he smiled. Then I made 'DAVY' in dough but he scrunched it up. At this point it occurred to me that he might accept words more easily if they were on the wall, so that his head was up (as when he was watching the TV), vertical instead of horizontal. Using fridge magnet letters I wrote 'Davy' on the metal board on the wall. He took the letters off at once, but then used them to spell 'Davy' himself on the board.

It is not always clear whether these words have meaning for him or if they are simply images floating in his mind which he is trying to fix through tactile sensation. However, sometimes he makes objects, again those which he has seen on TV, such as his extremely accurate representation of a pirate boat which he made while I was there. That this had meaning for him was evidenced when, after looking at it for a while, he pushed his finger through the side, making a hole and immediately destroying it. Apparently this was what he did before he 'sunk' his boat. Later his teacher sat with him as he worked on a new boat and drew it up on the wall as he did it. At one stage she got the number of masts wrong. He glanced up, grabbed her hand and corrected it on her drawing.

To summarize, in order to get Davy's attention we have to link his sounds with his movements – otherwise he is not able to make use of them to interact. But once he has realized that when he makes a sound he will get a response, especially in the form of a tactile stimulus, a bridge is established through which he can relate to other people. With Davy, as well as using Intensive Interaction, we need to be able to think about which bits of his sensory intakes have meaning for him – which can he take on board and interpret when his ability to process sound and vision are breaking up? If we link his sounds to movement and feeling, it is to be hoped that he will soon learn they can also be used for communication.

And we also found it helpful to look at his logic, even if it was not all immediately apparent. By placing myself in his world, what I saw was that there was a faint chance that he would invest letters with meaning when they were vertical rather than horizontal, so it would be easier to get him to work with them if they were placed in this dimension.

What made it possible to get through to Davy was putting myself in his position, letting myself be drawn into his sensory experience. I had to look through his eyes, listen through his ears, feel through his skin in my flesh, so that I could look out from his world viewpoint.

Autism manifests in different ways and we tend to think of it according to the particular ritualized behaviours which characterize an individual. But rather than revealing the person, these behaviours mask their personality. At the time I had met him, Davy had learned to retreat into his fixation with letters, even if this protection lasted only for a short while.

Niall

While he is using the play-dough, Davy can cut out those external stimuli which so plague him. On the other hand, Niall, who is a few years older than Davy, has developed no such coping strategies. I see him in a residential school. Either he huddles in the far corner of his room under the bed with a blanket over him and a pillow covering his head, or if he is downstairs, he winds himself under the seat between the stretchers of a chair with his nose pressed against the floor. He keeps his arms and hands under his T-shirt and resists any attempts to bring them out. When he is upset he cries and beats his head. In psychological terms he appears to be naked to sensory bombardment. Occasionally his support staff are able to get him to hand them crayons so that they can then use them to scribble. This is the extent of his cooperation and like Davy and his PECS, he seems to use it as a way of dealing with the world outside, rather than relating to it.

In order to try and make sense of Niall's behaviour one needs to read the accounts of what it feels like for a child with severe autism to go into fragmentation and take on board the confusion and pain that this involves. They say such things as 'everything fires at once', a description which accords with Ramachandran's 'autonomic storm'. Only when we look at the falling apart of sensory coherence can we begin to understand his contortions and the ferocity with which he presses the cartilage of his nose against the boards, seeking relief through pressure. By concentrating on this activity, he can exclude the painful sensory overload that is consistently described as tipping the brain into fragmentation, a process where incoming stimuli break up and which is both confusing and painful (Barron and Barron 1992; Temple Grandin quoted in the 1992 Channel 4 film *A is for Autism*; Lindsay Weekes quoted in BBC Radio 4 documentary, *Bridge of Voices*, date unknown).

This was one of the few times that when starting an intervention I have felt the situation was hopeless. Niall was not just psychologically but also physically withdrawn, so deeply separated that I simply could not see where to begin. However, together with Kelly, an assistant psychologist, we squeezed under his bed and started to respond to his very minimal breathing sounds and small noises by scratching the floor when he made any movement or sigh. After about half an hour he moved from hiding his head under the pillow turned away, to beginning to look out at us with his head propped on his arm and without his pillow for protection. For a short while his hand came out of his shirt to respond to Kelly's scratching noises by joining in. He began to relax and smiled a little.

With Niall on that first intervention, progress was signalled by such minute shifts in body language as to be almost unnoticeable. For Niall, his willingness to move out from under his pillow, even to bring his hands out, were major shifts indicating that he was starting to connect with what we were doing and desired to make contact. Such a small start. However, Kelly carried on in the consistent belief that it was worth continuing. She visited him daily, gradually wooing him out from his retreat, combining scratching the floor with other activities she discovered he enjoyed, such as blowing bubbles and singing 'Rudolph the Red-Nosed Reindeer', an activity which he began to join in. Progress was interrupted when she went on holiday, but a firm programme of interventions was put in place on her return and he started to improve again. She introduced finger painting and play-dough and his hands came out to use these. His eye-contact improved. His response to her next week's holiday was different. On her return he knew what he wanted, rushed her to the games room, grabbed her keys and opened the cupboard.

In that first session under the bed, I really had wondered if it would ever be possible to make headway with Niall. It was the persistence and creative way that Kelly continued to interact with him, using the language he understood even when he slipped back – and her faith in him – which has changed him from a deeply traumatized child to one who now interacts, laughs and is able to go home and stay with his mum for the weekend.

Alex

Alex again is different. He is seven and, unlike Davy and Niall, very large for his age and inclined to be aggressive to his family and support partners if he does not get what he wants. He has become extremely difficult to manage both at home and at school. I see him at home.

Although Alex has not yet had a formal diagnosis, I have included him among this group of children with autism, because there is little doubt in my mind that this is where he belongs. He finds change very difficult, has difficulties with new people and groups of people, has periods when he apparently does not know what is happening and a number of repetitive behaviours, such as flicking through magazines and turning light switches on and off. These are all difficulties which relate to processing information.

Alex puts his hands over his ears. (Sometimes this is an indication of hypersensitivity to sound, but it can also be an attempt to cut down the general volume of sensory intake, not just sound.) But he is quick to respond to my using his sounds and movements to communicate with him. For example, we tap different rhythms on the table. He pays attention, smiles and sticks his arm in the air. I do the same. He puts his hand on his head. I follow his lead. I rub my hair with my hand, he imitates me, rubbing his hair with his hand. We play with different positions and actions of hands on head. Alex both copies new movements made to him and introduces new actions himself, referring back to me to see what effect he is having, all basic steps towards learning to communicate. At this stage he is smiling and obviously enjoying our interactions – but then it becomes too much for him, too stimulating. Overwhelmed by his pleasure, Alex rolls over on the sofa and hides his head in his hands and peeps at me occasionally between his fingers.

Donna Williams (1996) describes this reaction as one of emotional overload, where the sensation that those of us who are not autistic (neurotypical) experience as emotional warmth, is one of pain. Temple Grandin says in the film *A is for Autism* that the person feels as if they are drowning in a tidal wave of unregulated sensation. This is too much and they retreat from it.

So when we play these games, we have to be careful not to overload Alex and get him too excited. I introduce his family to the idea of responding quietly to his initiatives in a way that is meaningful to him, so that he begins to share his activities. I suggest that when Alex looks at a catalogue, they sit by him with another and leaf through it as he does – and when he plays bubbles, they arrange to have two guns so that they can do it together. We need to work through any activities that people like because it holds their attention. For example, Alex likes cats and dogs, so his family can make scrapbooks with him of real pictures of cats and dogs, preferably doing things they can talk about (like cat sitting on a wall). I am suggesting that they try and make everything he does a vehicle for interaction.

Like many parents of children with autism, Alex's family are desperate for him to talk, and Alex does seem to want to communicate. He uses some Makaton and he can say a few words, such as 'cat', 'dog', and has an approximate try at some other words. I suggest that if he says a word or tries to say a word, 'tap his back' in approval. He also says 'No' a great deal in a way that suggests that this is a sound he has learned from the number of times it has been said to him to try and stop his difficult-to-manage behaviour. But in addition to speech or sign Alex is also very good at miming what he is trying to say. For example, he managed to communicate to his mother that he had seen a mouse in the back of the house by pointing to the floor in an erratic path and squeaking.

When we use his sounds and movements with him quietly, he seems to become calmer and more responsive to negotiation. He understands and responds better to requests. For example, Alex's soap-bubble gun was lost. He is very attached to this and the liquid soap bottles had been put away in the cupboard. He fetched them and tried to indicate to his mother by pulling her that he wanted the gun. He started to become agitated. His father took the bottles and hid them upstairs. Alex found them and brought them down and continued to indicate he wanted them by pulling at her. However, this did not escalate to a tantrum as we continued to use his sounds combined with gesture to say 'No'. He accepted this and put them away.

Another time, Alex took some food out of the fridge and showed it to his mother, indicating he wanted to eat it. She asked him to put it back, at the same time saying to me, 'There is no way that he is going to put it back in the fridge.' We continued to make his sounds, and he put it back in the fridge and shut the door. There is some way that using a person's own repertoire holds their attention in a world outside themselves and their inner desires, enabling them to respond in an appropriate way, not infrequently over-riding their hypersensitivities and 'difficult' behaviours. It is as if hearing their own language from 'out there' is so fascinating that the brain pays attention to it, almost in spite of its internal messaging.

One of the ways of helping people to be in touch with their lives is through negotiation, not doing things before we are absolutely sure that they understand what is going to happen and have indicated their agreement. Such agreement may be only a nod or a flick of the eyes, but while this is a matter of courtesy in all our dealings with each other, it is particularly important when we are trying to communicate with people on the autistic spectrum, because unexpected events can be so terrifying.

So at this stage we started to think how we could use negotiation to help Alex through what are for him critical situations where he loses track of what is happening. I suggested that when we tell him what we are going to do, we also use gestures that will show him how our action will end. (People on the autistic spectrum say we never finish our sentences. In particular, we say we are going somewhere but do not say we are coming back. This causes confusion in the brain.) So we need to tell him what we are going to do. For example, 'I am going upstairs to the toilet and then I am coming back down here again.' Our words are accompanied by pointing upstairs and then down to where we are currently standing. We wait for a nod that he has understood, repeating our communication if necessary.

We can apply this approach of negotiation to the rather more critical situation that sometimes arises when Alex's mother takes him out in the car and he hits her while she is driving because he wants to continue going out rather than coming home. The plan is to make sure that Alex knows what is going to happen before they start out by saying to him very clearly, 'Alex, we are going to Tesco's and then coming back again. Is that OK?' At the same time, his mother needs to point to the door, make the Makaton driving sign, which he understands and uses, and then point back to the floor where they are standing. Wait for a nod to see that he has understood.

When they have visited the shop, before they get in the car, she should tell him they are going home, combining words with gesture and his sounds, since it is better to work through this before starting to drive. The main thing is that his mother is letting him know what she is going to do before she does it and waiting for him to agree, so she knows that he knows exactly what is going to happen.

If he does start hitting in the car, she needs to stop, (a) because it is unsafe to continue, and (b) because she can then start to empathize and negotiate with him through his sounds. She should use these to calm him

down. (It's better to wait, even if it takes some time, since he does not
need to learn that if he goes on nagging you he will get his way.) If he
screams, she should make the same sounds softly and sympathetically.
When he is calm tell him what is going to happen and wait until he nods
agreement before driving home.

Alex's mother raises another problem. When they visit relatives who
live across the street, Alex gets very upset because he wants to get in the
car instead. Telling him where they are going is not enough, so I suggest
that he is given a weight to carry over the road to take to his auntie. His
mother fills up two carrier bags for him to carry, a simple strategy to give
him a point of focus. Concentrating on this weight he can now cross
straight over to the other side and into her house. Like Davy and his pot
full of play-dough, the weight speaks to him in a meaningful and contingent way that words do not. Paying attention to the weight, Alex is no
longer overcome by his internal confusion.

In terms of reducing the bombardment of sensory stimuli they are
unable to process, Davy, Niall and Alex have each developed a dominant
separate strategy, although they may resort to alternatives. Davy opts out
by focusing on his fixation, trying to make sense of the world outside
through his play-dough, his total concentration cutting out sensory input
from the outside world. Niall turns his back on the world, cutting out all
visual stimuli by hiding under a blanket and a pillow. If this does not
work, he does what amounts to self-harm, using the pain of pressure on
his nasal cartilage as a distraction. And if this does not work, he beats his
head. Alex's approach is different in that he can become aggressive
towards others; tactically he is trying to reduce the source of overload. All
these strategies have one aim, to stop the brain becoming overloaded and
forcing them into the painful and terrifying process of the autonomic
storm. The closer we get to them, the more easy it is to see what is
troubling their lives so that we can introduce strategies to help them deal
with it.

In the next chapter we briefly meet Di, a woman with cerebral palsy
who is in pain and crying, and Trish who also has cerebral palsy. Trish is
unwilling or unable to join in activities offered her in the day centre.

9

Cerebral Palsy

Posture

It is hard to communicate if one is in pain, so our difficulties in establishing contact may have a physical background, which needs to be addressed before we can gain our partner's attention. Just after I had started working in one of the old hospitals for people with learning disability I met Di, who had severe cerebral palsy and spent her days screaming. I was told she was attention seeking – that in some way she was winding people up. Thirty-five years ago this sort of attitude and language was acceptable. Fresh to my job, I did not question it until a new physiotherapist came and looked at her seating and arranged comfortable support for her twisted body. Her screaming stopped. Now it was possible to gather her attention.

There is increasing concern about the positioning of people with severe cerebral palsy and the postural difficulties that can be caused if it is untreated. Skeletal distortions and consequent pressure on the internal organs cause severe pain. The need for expert advice is still not always recognized but remains absolutely critical. In terms of training, help is available from the Postural Care Skills Programme, validated by the Open College Network based at Warwick University (www.posturalcareskills .com).

Meeting Trish

Trish also has cerebral palsy and learning disability. In her case she can walk, but she is non-verbal and extremely cut off. It is difficult to engage her attention for more than a few minutes. She fiddles with an activity for a short while, after which she will wander off and disrupt the activities of others in the day centre. She does not appear to be personally engaged, and at the end of the day her support worker, who tries hard to get her attention and offer her activities she might enjoy, is often disappointed, feeling she has been unable to get close to her at all.

There are some people with very severe learning disabilities who are so out of touch that one has to ask if this is because they are on the autistic spectrum, or if they are deaf, either physically or effectively. In the latter case it may be that since they have never received what their brain recognizes as a meaningful reply to their utterances, they have not made the connection between their attempts to communicate and the world outside. We have not answered them, so there is no bridge between their inside world and the world outside. They do not connect, and neither can we because they have not learned to listen and attend.

It can be difficult to tell the difference. Both appear unattached, but in my experience there is sometimes a difference in where their attention is – or is not. Looking carefully, a child on the autistic spectrum cannot be described as looking blank. In fact they are paying acute attention to some inner world or object, they are fixated or focusing on something, whereas the child whose problem is making an auditory link more often has an unattached floating vagueness.

Trish's lack of response and vacant look suggest that she may be at least partially effectively deaf if not physically, possibly because she is not used to receiving significant answers to her small sounds. Proceeding on this assumption, I tried using high sounds to respond to her. The effect was marked. She turned to me at once and smiled.

As the afternoon progressed and her brain got the idea that she would always get a response to her sounds, she appeared to hear over a rather wider range and her sounds became more frequent. Her attention shifted from her lost inner world to what was going on around her. She became more interactive and began to take notice of a range of other things, including the video camera. She was fascinated by seeing first myself and then her support partner on-screen. In both cases she deliberately stretched out her hand to touch us while she was also watching us perform, showing us that she clearly recognized the relation between what we were doing and what she saw. It was also an indication that she has good sight and could clearly pick out what was going on, on a small screen. We continued to explore what she could hear as indicated by what she responded to. At this stage it was suggested that we use balloons to amplify the sounds from our mouths to cause vibrations on her skin, a technique used with deaf children. Because there were no balloons we blew up disposable rubber gloves. At first Trish was nervous of these, so we used them to play a number of games with her.

Trish began to innovate. She picked up a crayon and handed it to us, so we drew faces on the balloons. She then added her own lines to the face, drawing on one, then on the other, at the same time turning her pen round so that it was correctly orientated. We played 'catch' and Trish was able to catch the balloon (a balloon moves more slowly than a ball so she has time to get her arms in the right position). She took her balloon to throw to other people including another service user. All the time her face was alert and lively, frequently smiling. Eventually she allowed us to place the balloon against her skin. At first we did it by making one of her sounds and then moving the balloon until it touched her face. Finally she was moving her head towards the balloon. She put her arm around her partner and leant her head against hers.

Judging by Trish's responses to the video camera, her capacity to pay attention and her acute interest in seeing herself and us on it indicated that she was much more able than her previous behaviour would suggest. Before we could attract her attention we had to penetrate the kind of miasma in which she lived. Our initial breakthrough was auditory, getting a pitch that she heard without difficulty. Once she recognized what we were doing she switched to being responsive to our interventions and replies.

Through the dedicated work of her support staff, Trish has continued to improve. She now pays attention to a variety of activities provided they are used as the basis of interaction. She is no longer withdrawn into an inner private world.

When we are working with people with cerebral palsy, we need to remember that it can take a very long time to organize their musculature and replies may be delayed. We have to wait and watch for responses.

Just as people on the autistic spectrum may present as more learning disabled than they actually are because of their withdrawal, so also people with the severe limitations imposed by cerebal palsy may do the same. And even people with learning disabilities may withdraw if they are only offered opportunities that seem to them without interest. I particularly recall one man, Reg, who appeared to have profound disability. He spent his time sitting in a chair, totally unresponsive to table top activities he was offered, until I fixed up an adapted game of table tennis. At this stage he came to life. I suggested that the staff introduce an activity such as helping to strip a motorbike. Even if he can only pass a spanner when asked he would be doing something that had meaning for him. Up until now this man had been so bored he had sunk into a sort of survival mode in his own world where he listened to himself. I had to start by using the sounds he made when he breathed in order to get in touch with him. The second day he had smiled and put out his hand to me.

With the exception of Nick, most of the people we have met so far have been young. How about age? Does getting old make any difference to the ability to respond?

10

Does Age Matter?

Most of the people we have met so far have been young. How about age? Does getting old make any difference to the ability to respond?

In some ways, working with adults on the autistic range is easier than with young children. Whereas a child tends to slither from one repetitive defence to another, in an adult the coping strategies which underpin their language are more sharply defined and therefore more easy to pick up. Histories differ – but in a number of people on the autistic spectrum, bonding of mother and infant and subsequent development may have gone smoothly until around the age of three. At this stage the door of communication slams shut. Parents suddenly find themselves with a small and sometimes destructive tornado on their hands, whirling through the house, climbing on everything, apparently obsessed by ritual behaviours and totally self-absorbed behind an invisible wall, unreadable and unreachable.

Most of his time the world of a small boy called Robert is defined by crisp packets. He wriggles their crackling shiny surfaces until they wear out and fall apart, scattering the contents all over the house. He is not interested in the fragments, only their container. He moves from this activity to watching a particular cartoon on the TV or climbing onto the narrow windowsill. He runs his fingers along the side of a laundry basket, feeling the bumpy woven plastic. In the chaos of his mind, these are the activities which his brain recognizes – 'When I do this I know what I am doing.'

I see him and his mother briefly, using his sounds. Her plight is as desperate as his, if in a different way. His responses are minimal until he is upstairs and we are still down. I 'answer' each of his sounds. When he comes down there is a gleam of mischief in his eyes as he runs through the room. However briefly, here is a child who has made a connection. It is learning to spot the 'connected moments' and work from these that bring possibility to his mother, refocusing her attention back to a way of being in touch with her child which comes naturally through the infant–mother paradigm.

We never know at the outset of this journey how far we can travel, there are so many factors to be taken into account. Not all relationships will progress as far as that of the deeply autistic virtually non-verbal child who, after a few months of using her body language with her, put her arms round her father's neck and said 'I love you' – but the communication established through this approach does offers hope. At least now there is a way we can learn to talk to each other in a way that has meaning for both of us.

As our partners get older, we might expect that they become more difficult to reach. However, looking back over work that has ranged with people aged from three to those in their sixties, I should say this is not so – but also that on reflection, I think the wrong question is being asked. We should do better to enquire as to an individual's life circumstances, bearing in mind that almost all the people who are now old have been in long-stay care. While this may have been a happy event, many who experienced it also experienced physical or sexual abuse. A person who has been abused will be afraid, and fear will colour their capacity to trust even a benign approach.

For some of the aged – and the not so old who have withdrawn completely or whose automatic response is one of aggression – it is more relevant to ask about how much trauma their life has brought them, rather than their chronological age.

Rosie

Rosie has severe learning disabilities. When I was first asked to see her in 2002, she was forty-nine. She was very withdrawn, curled up in an almost foetal position on the floor with her back to the wall. She had come to her present home about five months before and spent much of her time screaming and hitting herself. The adjectives used about her at this time were 'frightened' and 'disturbed', and it was observed that any personality she had was masked by her distress. The staff who supported her were loving and caring but felt they really had reached a point where they did not know what to do – 'We don't know where to go to help her.'

Since she developed cataracts, Rosie has had no effective sight. She has also had a bilateral stroke, which left her with little movement although this was returning slowly. It was difficult to know how able she was since there were gaps in her written history and there seemed to be no way of communicating with her. It was known that since she had left home in her twenties she had received little stimulus or affection.

Although Rosie could sit up, she did not like sitting in a chair, so getting her out to any form of activity seemed impossible. She was virtually housebound and in practice this meant that she stayed in her room. The question was whether the use of Intensive Interaction could help establish a link with her.

I sat with Rosie and watched her. Careful observation suggested that the way that she talked to her self (the inner language that her brain and body use to self-stimulate) consists of tapping her mouth area with her right fist and rubbing her finger and thumb together. More occasionally, she banged her feet on the floor, and made 'sh-sh-sh' sounds. In a world she very clearly had learned not to trust, these sensations were familiar to her. At least when she did them she knew what she was doing.

To begin with, I simply echoed her movement of face tapping by lying on the floor near her and banging the floor gently. Later I was allowed to do this on her left hand. I used her 'Sh' sound with her and she started to make others very softly, so softly that these were not immediately obvious and easy to pick up. However, she began to listen to my responses to her sounds and movements and started to smile. She was amused when I banged the floor near her legs when she banged her feet. In the second session, she took my hand and held it. The third took place in the hall, when she had apparently come out of her room, possibly looking for more – it seemed like that. I let her know I was there by clapping, and she sat up and placed her face very close to mine. The light was shining on my face from an overhead window. Perhaps she could see enough to distinguish between dark and light. When Rosie had had enough she let me know by turning away.

As usual, I explained to her care team that the way to connect with Rosie, at least to begin with, was to put aside 'our language' and respond to her through her body language, particularly through the rhythms which are part of her repertoire, using these to build up an intimate conversation. I also explained that the normal outcome of such an approach is to engender relaxation, trust and confidence, not only during sessions but also in the lives of our partners in general.

The practice that Rosie's team developed was outstanding, and I began to get feedback of a remarkable change in the quality of her life. So just over three years later I went back to see her, partly to check up, but more importantly to try and understand just how the change had been brought about and what part Intensive Interaction had played in this transformation. As I entered her house it was difficult to believe I was looking at the same person. Yes, she was in her room on the floor, but well away from the wall, and about to get dressed to go out in her wheelchair to a music group at the local college. She had a terrific grin on her face. She looked like someone who was enjoying herself. When she was asked if she would like to turn her radio down so we could talk she felt for the switch and giving a wicked laugh turned it up – not a mistake, she orientated herself towards us – she was teasing. She had a sparkle in her face, it was alert and lively. We talked about the activities, the swimming and trampolining she goes out to now that she is confident enough to use her wheelchair. At first when she got in the water she clung on, but now she stands by herself and splashes. She shares a lovely giggly relationship carried out in close proximity with her support partner.

Rosie is not on the autistic spectrum. It is not the difficulties in sensory processing that had led her into such a deeply entrenched defensive position – but fear. (If I keep my back to the wall or stay in bed I have a solid base which I understand. My body knows where it is and I am less likely to get hurt.)

So what has changed Rosie's life, turned it from a miserable existence, a fight for survival, into a vibrant minute-by-minute positive relationship? Top of the list has to be the love and respect shown by her support team who clearly value her way beyond a token attitude. But knowing this team, such courtesy was in place before, yet still, as Bruno Bettelheim said of children on the autistic spectrum, 'Love is not enough.' We still need skill, a skill which in this case involves going into Rosie's world (finding a way into the fortress she has built herself in order to protect herself from a world she perceives as hostile) and uncovering what it is that has significance for her. And this involves learning her language and using it with her, a sort of Trojan horse with benign intent.

In her previous placements it appears that Rosie had been seen as so difficult that people only interacted with her when they had to. So she had been changed and washed and fed and dressed and undressed, but that was it. There was a total lack of personal sensitivity, any sense that she mattered as a person, that valued her and what she experienced, that found her company worthwhile. Once we had identified how it was that Rosie talked to herself, which bits of her sounds and movements were meaningful for her, Rosie's team started to spend time with her answering all her initiatives. She understood very quickly that if she did something, her support partner would respond. Gradually she began to trust them – a slow business – and staff say they are still learning. (A healthy attitude – once we think we know it all, we close off any new avenues that may emerge. Growth doesn't just stop, it shrinks if we do not respond since we tell our partners we are no longer listening to them.)

But more happened. Because they were observing her so closely and were so closely involved with her, they began to read her body language more closely. Her team manager made what might appear to be a very simple observation when she observed: 'In this intimate conversation we noticed what she liked and disliked. We showed her this by respecting her preferences and because of this, she became more confident and trusting.' Simple or not, such an attitude is one of total regard for the individuality of the person, how *they* feel and what has significance for them at this present time rather than slotting them into a predetermined care programme, no matter how benign.

Although staff still use her sounds and tapping movements to communicate with her, and revert to these if she becomes disturbed, or use them to enhance their other communications, now she has got into the habit of listening and being listened to, they can talk to her using 'our language'. And now she is no longer afraid, she seems to understand most of it. Her sense of humour has emerged and her personality flowered.

After about six months of this personal intervention she is able to trust people enough to use the wheelchair. At first she would only use it to go out for walks, but now will sit in it when she returns – and in this way has learned to sit up in a chair instead of always lying on the floor. She uses her radio and has learned to control the switches, turning it off if it is playing music she does not like. She likes certain sounds – the rainmaker tube, the sound of a scrubbing brush on a hard floor and stripping velcro, incidentally all sounds similar to the 'sh-sh-sh' sound she makes. She enjoys her different-shaped bracelets and beads and likes to be told she is looking good. When you talk to her, she laughs and makes sounds back. She nods for 'Yes' and shakes her head for 'No'. She points for what she wants. At first she pointed anywhere, but now it is directional. She finds it helpful if people who are going away tell her they are coming back. She waves 'Goodbye' when she has had enough.

All these are small individual increments but add up to a complete and radical turn around for Rosie. She is now a happy woman, enjoying and taking part in her life.

The part played by Intensive Interaction was to open the door, not only for Rosie, but for us as well. It helped Rosie to attend. She enjoyed interaction and looked for more, but it also helped us to get to know the lovely lively 'person' who was at home, who could respond and with whom we could enjoy interaction.

Jeff

Jeff is even older, in his sixties. He has been in institutions all his life. He has Down's syndrome and presents as puzzled and anxious, always on the alert, looking round to see what is happening. He also has a very low threshold for feeling threatened and becomes upset frequently, pinching or throwing objects. Some of his behaviour suggests he may be on the autistic spectrum. There is a suggestion that he is showing signs of dementia. Meeting him, it is clear that it is going to be hard to bring change at this late stage and show him a more relaxed way of living.

Although non-verbal, Jeff can communicate his needs and is upset if these are not met. Apart from this, he tends to keep himself very much to himself and any interaction and responses are minimal. He does like the feeling of being outdoors and will smile to himself when he feels the wind.

Jeff understands speech and seems to know what is required, although he may not wish to do whatever is asked. He seems to be afraid if things happen too close to him suddenly. He needs to know what is happening. (Living as we do in a different sensory reality, it is difficult for us to take on board that for some people, this 'suddenly being faced with an unexpected situation' may be completely life-threatening in that it triggers the fight/flight defence system.) In order to help him with this it is important that before they do something, staff need to stand off, tell him what they are going to do and ask if this is all right. It is crucial that time is given for him to reply.

In order to give Jeff a positive way of saying 'No' we need to give him the opportunity to do so. For example, when I first came in he was sitting at a table. I stood at the far side, pointed to the chair and said, 'May I sit down?' He nodded, so I sat down. If he had shaken his head, I should not have done so. The point of this approach is that it allows him to join in his life and take responsibility and control of what happens. His agenda of 'needing to know what is happening' is more important than ours of 'getting him to do something'. What seems to be happening at present is that he *is* asked, but no time is given to let him answer before the action takes place – so the only way he has of saying 'No' is to pinch.

So often we ask someone if they would like a cup of tea and hand it to them before they have had time to reply. Giving a person time to indicate 'No' allows them to have some say in their lives. The more they can be persuaded to respond through nods rather than things just happening to them, the better.

It is difficult to introduce Intensive Interaction to Jeff as he is clearly suspicious of me and also there were a lot of people watching him. Jeff has lived much of his life in long-stay hospitals. We do not know exactly how his fearfulness arose but it is seen in people who have been institutionalized and it makes it more difficult to reach them since engagement appears to be threatening. Even getting physically close to him arouses suspicion. I use his sounds and rocking movements together and his posture suggests he is 'listening'. He responds better to his key-worker with whom he is familiar, taking her hands and rocking with her. I suggest that at the same time she moves his hands up and down to emphasize the rhythm of his movements.

Senescence

Using Intensive Interaction with people who are suffering from Alzheimer-related dementia, Astell and Ellis (2006) work with the still-face technique and demonstrate clearly, that although the ability to converse fluently may no longer be present, the desire to communicate is still functional. Jessie is a seventy-nine-year-old lady with severe Alzheimer's. Her speech is muddled and limited, which leads to her being excluded from normal social exchange. During a coded session, both partners used imitation (verbal and non-verbal) to keep communication on track. When Jessie moved her hands, her partner mirrored this and Jessie immediately looked at her and smiled. A connection was made.

Even in senescence there is increasing evidence that when our capacity to communicate is falling apart, imitation is still a doorway to communication. Visiting a close friend with dementia in the last weeks of her life, she no longer recognized me. Her fingers were scratching her bedclothes. When I scratched the same rhythm on her sheet, she paused and attended. It may not sound much, but for us, even though her cognitive faculties had perished, we were able to rejoin each other in affect, through an imitative act that was meaningful to both of us. Fleetingly, it brought us together again, meeting for the last time.

11

Changing Rooms

The behaviour of a person on the autistic spectrum can vary widely from one context to another. An individual who is deeply distressed in one place may be calm and responsive in another. But when a person is disturbed, it may be very difficult to shift the prevailing mindset of their care providers from 'control' to understanding, from seeing them as 'attention seeking' and sometimes violent, to asking themselves why the person is so upset that they resort to aggression.

It is important for us to remember that autism is reactive. *How* it manifests itself is a product not only of the condition of autism but also of the environment to which it is exposed. For example, it is increasingly recognized that certain sensory stimuli are painful and lead to disturbed behaviour. Some people on the spectrum are extremely hypersensitive to light. In their efforts to avoid sitting in a desk looking out of a window, a child may become very distressed and disturbed. Similarly with sound, certain frequencies are acutely painful.

But in addition to hypersensitivity, some solutions are caused by layout. How can we re-arrange an environment so that those events that upset a person are reduced or extinguished? First of all we need to identify the triggers for particular behaviours. We must learn to substitute the attitude 'Why does he need to do this?' for 'How can we control this?'

Most environments in which people live are accidental. They are not planned to meet the particular difficulties they may be experiencing. In such cases we may quite inadvertently be setting up the triggers for this individual's aggression. People who feel that those they support should 'get used to it', whatever the situation is, are overlooking the brain dysfunctions which distort the perception of what neurotypical people see as normal (and therefore 'the norm' to which everyone should conform). We should never forget that the sensory experience of people on the autistic spectrum is different. Even for a neurotypical, we are all different, mine is not the same as yours – and if you are reading this, neither of us is experiencing the same reality as some of those we support. This is true whether they have multiple disability or are on the autistic spectrum. If we are deaf, we may get muddled messages. Shouting does not cure our confusion. We will need help which pays regard to our disability.

Bill

Bill is young man with ASD. He spends much of his time locked in his inner world, playing with a piece of paper or a crisp bag which he likes to tear and post through a lattice fence. (This type of object is known as a 'stim', derived from its use, a 'stimulating object'.) This can easily be converted into a shared activity by taking another piece of paper and posting it with him. He becomes playful, interactive and smiling. The day we meet is windy. We enjoy a great game together when I try and catch his papers in a box. He is falling about laughing. Both of us are learning about the pleasure of having fun together. His sounds, which are quiet at first, become clearer. As he quickly realizes that if he makes a sound he will get a response, he makes different ones, looking to see what effect it has on me. Now that he is communicating in a way that has meaning for him, he is liberated from his self-interest and wants to know what I will do. He is interested in me, what I think of his utterances. This capacity to refer back is at odds with the prevalent view that people on the autistic spectrum are not interested in the reactions of others. What is different here is that we have been able to make connection through significant signals his brain recognizes.

However, when Bill comes back from the walk he has enjoyed into his house, he makes a nosedive for the waste bin and drags out a piece of paper to flap. Because it has come from the bin it is taken away from him, since it is regarded as dirty. Denied the object (stim) on which he can focus to the exclusion of overloading stimuli he becomes distressed and starts to kick the furniture. He is restrained and guided to the garden where staff try to divert his attention by kicking a football (an activity he sometimes enjoys). He is not drawn out from his distress. Instead of cooling off, he tries to enter another bungalow where it is feared he will attack another resident or their property. So he is taken and guided by two staff towards his bedroom. I am told that the normal outcome of this practice is that, once in his room he will break things, self-harm and hit the pictures on his wall.

Working with distressed behaviour involves looking not just at what immediate action we take, but also what it is that is triggering their distress. In this case, in order to unravel why has Bill changed so suddenly from enjoying being on a walk to behaviour which is distraught, we need to look at the geography of the house as well as his reactions.

When Bill comes in from his walk he comes in through the back door into a noisy kitchen with people milling about, an area of high sensory bombardment. He feels himself becoming sensorily overloaded. He tries to obtain a 'stim', in this case an empty biscuit packet from the bin. He seeks reassurance in an activity that is 'hard-wired in'. He is now involved in an activity which is familiar, so he does not feel threatened by the possibility of fragmentation with all its confusion and pain. Focusing on this helps him to cut down on the external overload.

The trigger for this particular outburst is when Bill is stopped from obtaining his stim. He is not allowed to have the one thing which will decrease the disturbed brain patterns which are so painful.

So what is it wrong with a room (or a playground) full of people?

Jolliffe et al. (1992) tell us that people are the most difficult of all, since the brain has to process the shape, movement and sounds simultaneously. It is quite literally overloaded. The images and sounds and tactile sensations break up. Many people on the autistic spectrum find that processing the sensory input that arises from the multiple demands of people – just their sheer presence, constantly changing shapes and incomprehensible language, and the complexity of the stimuli they present – is the most difficult situation they have to deal with, to the extent that they cut themselves off completely.

When Bill walks through the door into the kitchen he is met not only by a different scenario, but one that is full of people, moving, shape-changing and noisy. Afraid of tipping into the distressing and painful process known as fragmentation, where the sensory input breaks up, he very sensibly tries to desensitize himself in the only way he knows how, by grabbing a 'stim' from the nearest place he knows there will be one – in the rubbish bin.

Gillingham (1995) tells us that if we prevent people from using self-stimulus we leave them vulnerable to sensory overload. When his paper is removed from him on the grounds that it is unclean, Bill is thrown back into the chaos and also the threat of fragmentation. He immediately starts kicking a kitchen cabinet and is consequently restrained.

At this point I suggest that instead of taking him to his room he is given a crisp packet. He calms down at once. Now he can focus on this, he is no longer under threat. However, rather than leave him in his own solitary world, a member of staff starts to interact with him at the fence with another piece of paper. Now he is not just calm but actively enjoying himself again.

Although he is now back to his repetitive behaviour, his attention has been switched from his internal distress to the world outside, from an internal retreat to an activity he can have fun sharing with his communication partner. He is now involved in a safe experience which his brain has no difficulty in processing, so it does not carry the threat of possible overload but is now an activity he shares.

The approach using our partner's personal body language which we know as Intensive Interaction does not stand by itself. Neither is it just about crisis management. It should be used as an ongoing process to maintain connectedness so that our partner always has a point of reference to maintain coherence.

Reflection on this particular outburst suggested that it was triggered by the layout of the house and the events which accompanied Bill's entrance. The back door leads straight into a busy kitchen which is the centre of activity in the house and always has several people in it. At this time, by great good fortune, the providing service was about to alter the house for unrelated reasons, so there was the opportunity to look at the plans and see if it is possible to address some of the problems which the building itself presented to its residents.

First of all it appears that although customary, it is not necessary to bring residents straight into the busy kitchen. Instead, they could use the front door which up until now has been virtually unused. This leads into a quiet passage. At the same time, Bill's key staff can give him a 'stim' so that when he changes his surroundings from the garden to the hall, he can focus on the paper and not feel drowned by a flood of new visual stimuli. This change and the use of Intensive Interaction with him has reduced the number of recorded incidents by more than half.

Upstairs there is another problem that related to the building, Bill likes baths but hates having a shower. Gerland (1996) tells us that for her, because of her hypersensitivity to touch, a shower feels like hot needles stabbing the skin. It really hurts. Unfortunately Bill also has a problem with time. Waiting for the bath to be available upsets him. One can imagine two unprocessed contradictory messages swirling round the brain: 'I am going to have a bath' and 'The bath is not happening'. Again this results in confusion and threatens break-up, with all the fear that brings in its wake. With this in mind it was decided to try and resolve the problem by changing one of the shower rooms into a second bathroom. Fortunately, this decision coincided with refurbishment work on the house. Since the installation of a second bath, his behaviour which was seen as challenging has disappeared.

Hypersensitivities cause pain. People who experience them do not get used to their affects. We need to be aware that if we place them in an environment which triggers overload and fragmentation then we are responsible for their distress and outbursts.

Behaviour we see as challenging is very often our fault. When looking for resolution, not only do we need to improve communication and help the person to feel good about themselves through Intensive Interaction but we also have to address the need to provide an autism-friendly environment.

As a result of this in-depth look at the roots of his distressed outbursts, staff begin to look differently at what has been seen up to now as 'challenging' behaviour. Rather than feeling the need to control him and in addition to talking to him through the language his brain recognizes, they now look for the trigger which has upset him to see if his circumstances can be modified. Bill is now leading a calmer and more interactive life.

12

Lost Voices, Learned Language

Whatever our state, we take it for granted that others experience the same as we do. It is one thing to be aware in our heads that another person's experience differs from our own, quite another to take this on board and understand what their experiences feel like, how different their perceptions are in the flesh, and how those which may be perceived as user-friendly in ourselves may actually be so threatening to them as to trigger the body's self-defence system.

Nowhere does this come adrift so easily as when the autistic and non-autistic worlds try to communicate with each other through the two principle channels of interaction, vision and speech. In Chapter 2 we saw how easy it is to misunderstand eye-contact or lack of it; in this chapter we are going to look at the difficulties that can arise with the use of spoken language. How does it feel in the mind when sounds keep dropping in and out, the constant effort to keep track and always the threat looming that the brain will simply pack up when the stress or pain becomes too great? How is it that speech, which for the neurotypical is the great facilitator, can be so great an obstacle, an impediment throwing our partner back into their inner world.

A parent says of his child, who is very disturbed and self-harming, 'I don't understand. He can talk, so why should we use non-verbal language with him?' And yet, in spite of having learned to talk, his ability to comprehend speech may be, at best, intermittent. Words that sound like hammering may merge and slip away all together. Keeping track of what is going on may be extremely stressful – even for those at the able end of the spectrum. Trying to talk him down when he is upset is precisely the way to lead him more deeply into confusion. So the question is, are there circumstances in which the use of non-verbal body language can help us keep in touch with people who have some speech? Surely this would be a backward step?

To answer this question we need to understand that during our acquisition of language, there are a number of stages at which the process can go down the wrong track. I want to look at a few here.

We feel isolated from people who cannot talk to us and bend all our efforts to make it possible for us to get in touch with each other. From our point of view, this is how we shall get to know them, not just what they need or want, but who they are. Teaching our partner non-verbal needs-based language systems that enable them to communicate what they need (such as PECS) is in some ways the easy bit. It does not tackle the problem of how they can express themselves if they still feel tongue-tied when it comes to feelings.

Mary

Meet Mary, a child with autism. She is very easily upset and can self-harm, hitting herself and being aggressive towards others. She has some language, so the question we need to address is, will using her body language, movements and sounds to connect with her help to reduce her evident stress, and if it does, will it also affect her ability to use our language? Should we not just plunge on and try and improve her verbal understanding?

Listening to Mary, although she uses phrases in appropriate places, there is something very odd about the use she makes of language.

Mary's mother tells us she heeded the advice she received and used very simple language with her, such as 'Put coat on'. Mary is able to say these phrases. For example, at mealtimes she will say, 'Put in mouth' – and repeat this over and over again, a sort of stutter in the mind, until whoever is her partner at the time says it back to her. Only then is she is able to open her mouth and eat. She seems unable to proceed to a relevant action without hearing her utterance repeated. If this is not done, she quickly becomes disturbed and throws her food around. The way she uses her speech sounds is as if the need to say it has become 'part of the task', rather than a description of it. In effect the speech has become an impediment to performance. It simply brings her to a full stop.

To understand what is going on here we need to look at our earliest communication process, one that we have all been through. If we watch mothers and babies we see that when the infant says something, 'Boo', the mother answers, 'Boo' and after a while the baby produces another sound, for example, 'Da'. In other words, the baby initiates, the mother confirms and the baby moves on. What seems to have happened in Mary's case is that she has got stuck at (or reverted to) a stage where she needs a mother or mother figure to confirm her utterance before she is able to complete the task and move on. Even when she is upset and desperate to get into her 'safe room' in order to reduce the overloading stimuli, she runs to it and stands outside saying 'safe room', waiting for someone to repeat this to her, to give her permission so to speak, before she can let herself in. Similarly, when she wants to hide under her blanket she will say 'blanket' and wait, becoming increasingly upset until someone has repeated it back to her so that she can then move on to hide. Each time she needs someone to confirm her before she can move on to complete an activity.

It's not that we are trying to reduce her command of our language – far from it – but as it is at present a cause of frustration which leads to aggressive outbursts we need to try and relocate it in such a way that it helps rather than hinders communication and action. The question we have to ask ourselves is how we can disengage her from this hiccup in her mental process?

What is suggested is that, at the point where her verbal processes are getting stuck, we use Mary's non-verbal sounds with her to try and free-up the log-jam that is currently being caused by her brain's misplacement of our language. Using a person's own body language to communicate with them does not require interpretation. Through the activity of the mirror neurones, the brain recognizes and latches on to elements of its own repertoire immediately. Quite how this is accomplished is not known, but in practice attention is shifted away from the bottleneck in the brain to the task in hand. So, for example, when Mary is eating and says 'Put in mouth', her partner uses one of her non-verbal 'ah' sounds to reply; so they might say 'Aaaahh, put in mouth', gradually reducing the interaction to 'aaahhh' without the instruction. What we are doing is using her body language as a non-invasive approach to free her from reliance on external confirmation, making a link with her in a way that is non-threatening because it does not need translation – and encouraging her to move on by herself. At present for Mary, although language is telling us what she wants to do, it is also a stumbling block that is preventing her from proceeding.

And what is interesting is, when we tried this she ate her food without getting upset, and as she relaxed, she learned my name (not one she is likely to have come across before) and used it appropriately to summon me.

Seven weeks later and the staff have been using Mary's sounds with her. The number of recorded outbursts of distressed and aggressive behaviour have dropped by over a third. When she becomes upset, as staff work with her sounds and rhythms she now becomes calm within a few minutes rather than up to half an hour. At meals, when she says, 'Put in mouth', some staff find it possible to move her on simply by nodding rather than having to repeat what she has said. Her use of our language has improved without prompt from her partners – instead of saying for example, 'Get in pool' she will say, 'Get in *the* pool'. She is using more words appropriately and attempting others. Three months on, she is using language much more specifically to ask for what she wants. For example if she is hungry she no longer just says she wants cheese (which she did no matter what food she wanted) but will say exactly which food it is she requires. Although she sometimes still hits out at staff, they say it is more half-hearted; generally she is more friendly and will take their hand. She uses the toilet more frequently – an indication that she is making more sense of her environment. If she is upset, she will take herself off to the blue room. Recently she attended a barbecue and walked round looking at people's faces as if she was interested in them.

Adopted personae

Starting at the beginning, words are like jars. It is difficult for those of us who are fluent to understand that they can be full of meaning – or alternatively they are just sounds, empty of content and context. We are so desperate to get our partners on the autistic spectrum to talk and to relate to what we say, that sometimes we force-feed them – they learn words without meaning. This is very misleading because we think they understand us and derive the same meaning as we do from a word. The simplest example is when they use 'time' words, such as 'soon' or 'later', but clearly have no clue as to the intervals involved.

So listen to what Donna Williams, who has severe autism, has to tell us about processing language. She was talking about how she thinks on

Channel 4 television in 1995. 'I could think of a table as a square, flat, brown, thud, thing with lines on it but not get from there to calling it "table", or from there to its context – a table is a thing you put plates on' (Williams 1995). Images without names or context – people on the spectrum can build up lexicons of unprocessed sensory impressions which they find difficult to make into words, to interpret these words into meaning and to relate the words to meaning and put the meanings into context. They say that living in a world that always demands interpretation sets up a war in the head and it is easier to retreat into themselves.

In his interesting book *Send in the Idiots*, Kamran Nazeer, himself on the spectrum, describes how his friend Andre dealt with this confusion (or, as others name it, fuzziness or blur) by building himself puppets to talk through. If he felt himself becoming overloaded, at first he would seek what he calls 'local coherence' through familiar and repetitive activities such as 'making patterns with his fingers on the bar', or other forms of fingertip stimulation on which he could focus and in doing so exclude surplus stimuli.

I think that when Andre talks about the need for local coherence he is referring to the situation when he feels his grasp of what is happening beginning to fail – and knowing the brain is slipping concentrates simple repetitive activities that help him to maintain control. If this level of protection against overload fails, he moves on to his secondary defence, substituting the puppets for himself. Although he is capable of conversation and, when he is speaking as himself can tolerate interruptions to his flow, when the puppets are speaking he becomes extremely angry if they are interrupted. Nazeer suggests that he uses the puppets to exclude intimacy.

If we think of emotions as internal sensory stimuli, they can be experienced as overwhelming surges of sensation, as Donna Williams (1996) describes. In the autistic brain, with its floating, unprocessed and conflicting fragments, Andre's puppets seem to offer a holding space for the unmanageable, but to do so requires extreme concentration. The trouble with such holding programmes is that eventually the emotion resurfaces and takes off. It is not surprising that Andre becomes distraught when this last bastion falls and he is left defenceless, swept away by rage.

Being able to talk is not necessarily a solution when the brain is overtaken by a tidal wave of affect. Under these circumstances they may project their 'bad self' on to something outside themselves. Communications no longer serve our partners as a link to the outside world but trap them in their inner world, either in a developmental stage or in a projection, one that expresses their 'bad' feelings. From the point of view of communication, the trouble with these 'displaced' communications is that the 'outside world' takes them at face value for what they are saying instead of considering their implications for an affective state.

This is how George Vaillant, Professor of Psychiatry at Harvard University opens his book *The Wisdom of the Ego*:

> Our lives are at times intolerable. At times we cannot bear reality. At such times our minds play tricks on us. Our minds distort inner and outer reality so that the observer might accuse us of denial, self-deception or even dishonesty – but such mental defences creatively rearrange the sources of our conflict so that they become manageable and we may survive. The mind's defences – like the body's immune mechanisms – protect us by providing a variety of illusions to filter pain and allow self-soothing. (Vaillant 1993)

When it comes to character, we are all a pick and mix of good bits and bad bits, and to some extent present ourselves differently in different circumstances. If there is too much pain in our lives, our brains devise strategies that protect us. If we are vulnerable, we may find it too painful to cope with the feelings that come from connecting with the world around us.

Under these circumstances we may protect ourselves by adopting a persona from some individual we meet, a persona that both facilitates connection but also shields us from having to expose our self.

('I know you think I am bad because I keep getting things wrong and I'm frightened so I do things wrong but I don't want to be bad. So it's not me that's bad but something outside me which is not me that does them.')

The trouble with this rationale is that when a person is separated from their bad feelings they do not feel responsible for them, so they are liable to burst out in unmanageable aggressive acts. When we meet people who have adopted such strategies, we can hear their different voices which they use to cope with a range of situations. In addition to the variety of voices they use to address different situations, they are often intensely interested in their reflections in the mirror.

> The task of splitting is to alleviate ambivalence and assign all good feelings to one person and all bad feelings to a scapegoat, A world that is approximately grey is separated into black and white

and the individual is left divided against themselves. (Vaillant
1993)

People on the autistic spectrum may experience internal affective
sensations (that a person who is neurotypical senses as mildly pleasurable
or distasteful) as extremely and even intolerably painful. So how does a
parent cope when a child is remote, sometimes destructive or
self-destructive and given to 'temper tantrums', or perhaps most difficult
of all, when the child attacks a brother or sister. However good our
parenting is, it is very easy for such children to learn that (since they may
not be able to make the subtle distinction between their negative activities
and their negative feelings) what they actually feel is 'bad', a bad that is
unacceptable. At first sight behavioural programmes offer a way of letting
the child know what is or is not acceptable. So what will be the effect of
such a programme which reinforces the feelings of an autistic child who is
experiencing emotional overload and is hypersensitive to his or her
internal sensations?

Josh

Meet Josh. If Mary was stuck in a developmental loop, Josh has a problem
which is perhaps more complex since, although his speech is clear, from
the way he uses it, it appears that he is rejecting part of himself.

Josh is eight. He has speech and expresses himself clearly. Recently he
has been placed on a behavioural programme designed to help him dis-
tinguish between what is good and what is bad behaviour. But his mother
is worried because he no longer seems to be talking to her, she feels she is
losing touch with him. Instead, he has taken to expressing himself
through a conversation between his hands, one known as 'Pal', the good
guy, and the other as 'Mr Hands', the bad guy.

For example, going upstairs to have a bath, Pal will say, 'I'm going to
have a bath', to which Hands will reply, 'I don't want to have a bath.' (Pal
does what his mother wants while Mr Hands says what he feels.) This
may seem harmless enough, but already Josh is splitting off those feelings
which he experiences as unacceptable. This way, they are not his responsibility. There is also a third voice, that of 'Dolly', the victim, the one who
suffers when it gets thrown downstairs or drowned in the bath.

I think that Josh's mother, who is extremely perceptive, is right to be
concerned, since not only are she and Josh failing to connect but also the

dispossession of negative feeling is leading to explosive outbursts of disturbed or self-harming behaviour when the feelings eventually surface. What we need to try and do is to bring bad guy and good guy back together and help Josh to understand that they are parts of himself and he is still loved, all of him (even if some aspects of his behaviour are difficult). Otherwise Josh is heading in the direction of split personas with all the complications this entails.

But where is real Josh? How can we get through to him without emotionally overloading his system? It is extremely difficult to know which bit of him to address. Pal seems to have disappeared and Mr Hands has become very aggressive towards Josh, hitting him. (I suspect that in Josh's desperate efforts to be good, Pal has joined forces with Mr Hands and collectively they have become the 'Controller', which is why Pal has disappeared.) The only clue we have to Josh's behaviour is that he is saying 'Shut up' to his mother when she speaks to him.

How can we try and unravel this? Going back to first principles, perhaps when Josh is telling his mother to shut up, what he is actually trying to say is, 'I can't cope with speech, it is overloading me.' At first since his personae are the most obvious features of his behaviour, I am lured into trying to address them directly, talking to Mr Hands or Pal, but this simply upsets him more (probably at least in part because interpreting speech in itself is the problem and adding more deepens the problem). However, addressing a projection directly – no matter how seductive it is – is like trying to engage with a hologram or a reflection which slips away through the fingers, a transparency that in itself it has no substance, no connection with real Josh. So I suggest to Josh's mother that she tries using his non-verbal sounds to connect with him. This process is ongoing, but she tells me that now when he gets upset she is able to calm him through empathetic use of his sounds. The next stage is to try using these with him when he is not upset, building them in to normal conversation so that it becomes part of the way she talks to him and he has 'markers' on which he can focus if he starts to become overloaded. She tells me she is becoming more confident in using his non-verbal sounds to engage, and Josh now enlists his mother's help when he feels Mr Hands is bullying him.

It does feel strange to address a person who has speech in non-verbal language since although we are ourselves monitoring the body language of those we talk to all the time, we are not used to doing this consciously.

Nevertheless, we only have to sit in a café and watch two people chatting over a cup of coffee. What we will hear and see is nods, head shakes, agreement 'mmm', clicks of the tongue, 'tt-tt', surprise, 'oh' and so on, affective sounds of attunement, just letting each other know they are still onside. Next time you talk to a friend, notice how often they nod in agreement. (This is a bit like both partners holding a piece of string at each end when they are talking and every now and then giving it a tweak, keeping in touch with each other, empathetic contact without the difficulties of interpretation and emotional overload.)

We also need to look at trying to reconnect Josh with his body. Sensory Integration points towards the need for deep body stimulation felt internally, in this case particularly connected with the hands – daily deep hand massage accompanied by direction towards the part of the hand which is being rubbed, the fingers, the nails, the joints, the palm, the wrist, in an almost anatomical way. This should be followed by an activity he likes, such as banging nails into a piece of wood, something that will bring to his attention the integrated use of hands (Jane Horwood, personal communication).

Sandra

The next history is that of Sandra. Her strange use of language also has psychological roots rather than structural. She has an immensely complicated background, and her difficulties are by no means resolved – but I want to include her because our meeting led me to understand more clearly how it is that the use of body language speaks to us, or rather which part of our psyche it addresses.

Sandra is in her late thirties. She has reasonable speech and can say what she wants. On first meeting her she presents as cheerful with a loud slightly wooden-sounding voice. I am asked to see her because her outbursts of aggression erupt suddenly and she lashes out at both staff and service users in the day centre she attends. Sandra has learning difficulties, and while she has not received a diagnosis of autism, some of her behaviour suggests that she may be on the spectrum. Some of the causes of her distress are obvious but her support staff do not find it easy to relate her other outbursts to what is going on round her.

Sandra's support staff are sensitive to her difficulties and know she is easily upset by any event which happens unexpectedly. Sudden loud sounds, such as balloons bursting, doors slamming and motor-cycles revving or backfiring, upset her, but so also does an event like banging herself on something. Over and above the pain, it can set off a train of self-harm where she bangs herself.

The two members of staff who work directly with Sandra also know that she has great problems with her feelings that people are invading her personal space. She is easily upset if people come too close. They have arranged for her to sit in a corner behind a table so that she does not easily feel directly threatened. She finds it particularly difficult if people are behind her such that she does not know what they are doing, although she manages quite happily if close contact is related to personal care and she knows exactly what is going to happen.

Sandra spends much of her time looking at herself in a mirror. She moves her head to see herself from different angles and sometimes it seems to me that it is almost as if she were 'flirting' with her image. It emerges in conversation with staff that, in addition to her bright cheerful voice, she sometimes mutters in a low growly aggressive tone. She seems to have two voices. Listening to her cheerful one has a quality about it which sounds slightly detached. I get the feeling that this is how Sandra has learned it is acceptable to communicate. She uses her negative one to swear and threaten, or in some instances to try and control her aggression. As I heard it, she muttered, 'I'm not going to hit Phoebe, I'm not going to hit her.' Her fists were clenched and she really was trying very hard to keep herself from doing what her feelings were urging her to do – to lash out at me whose behaviour she perceived as upsetting her.

Sitting with Sandra, two strands emerge in her behaviour. As mentioned above, she really cannot bear it when something unexpected happens. She is so sensitive that even turning away from her when one has been engaged in conversation may be enough to trigger an outburst. Her defence system is on a hair trigger. Whereas she knows what is happening if she is engaged in conversation, her world picture drops to pieces if the speaker then (apparently) abandons her. She does not know what is happening, triggering a feeling of being threatened, so she responds as if she is being attacked.

It is terribly difficult for us to appreciate quite what it means to have a defence system permanently on red alert. We know that some of us will be afraid of things which others are not. But what if the information provided by our senses is scrambled and constantly informing us that we are in mortal danger? Sandra's responses are in no way 'attention seeking' but more in the nature of a reaction to imminent global disaster. If something goes 'BANG', meaning drops out of her understanding and she is catastrophically lost. And again, if someone is too close or behind her, she does not know what is going to happen and feels herself to be under attack.

Like Andre and Josh, the second feature of Sandra's behaviour is that her two voices appear to reflect two different sides of her personality. In effect she has split off what she has learned is her 'bad' unacceptable side and in doing so has lost contact with her real self, how she feels herself to be. She tries to make contact with it when she talks to herself through the mirror – and also tries to control it (unfortunately sometimes unsuccess-fully) when she notices her negative feelings are getting out of control.

The ability to hide behind the shield of separated fragments of our personality can make a person very difficult to reach. As pointed out above, we may not know where they are, so we may think we are talking to the person without actually getting through to them in any meaningful way, in the sense that we reach their feeling level. Again, the problem is how can we find the 'real' Sandra when this self is hiding in a cocktail of adopted personae which present themselves (different facets for different occasions) as an extremely effective shield to prevent us getting through to the level of her feelings?

Some aspects of Sandra's behaviour sent me back to re-read Donna Williams' autobiography, *Nobody Nowhere* (1999). This is an extremely illuminating account of the journey into the adoption of false selves, an insider's view of how it feels to be so drawn into a character that one becomes that character. I have dwelt at length on it to try and shed light on what I had already observed in Sandra.

Much of the early part of *Nobody Nowhere* is taken up with how Donna develops and eventually adopts different personae, who represent different aspects of herself; on the one hand, her negative traits that protect her from having to interact directly with the world outside which is too painful, and on the other, her positive side enabling her to interact through the agency of a desired and desirable role model. (How naturally we use the phrase, 'on the one hand…and on the other' – small wonder that Andre and Josh instinctively use their hands to personify alternative personas.)

In a very brief introductory paragraph Donna tells us that her book is the story of two battles, the battle to keep out 'the world' and the battle to join it. There is the same ambiguity in Sandra as she tries to engage with 'our world'.

Donna's first character is Willie. At three, she says, she loses herself in Willie and 'becomes' him. He protects her because people are frightened of him. Her negative characteristics have become a separate entity. 'Willie became the self I directed at the outside world, complete with hateful glaring eyes, a pinched up mouth, rigid corpse-like stance and clenched fists. Willie stamped his foot, spat and had a look of complete hatred...Donna paid the price.'

Donna's next alter ego (adopted self) is Carol. She meets a child called Carol in the park just once and goes home with her. Carol's home circumstances compare so favourably with her own (where her mother rejected her and father drank) that Donna longs to be Carol and becomes so wrapped up into her that in her mind she becomes Carol, or rather Carol becomes Donna.

From now on, Donna meets Carol through the mirror. There follows a long description of how she tried to walk through the mirror to find Carol and her house. She says that she spent four years trying to get through by walking into the glass. She retreats to the cupboard in despair and then finds Carol inside herself. She becomes like her, speaks, laughs, makes friends. Her mother is pleased that 'Donna' has disappeared.

But in learning to function through copying other people, Donna 'loses her own body language, uses different voices and her life becomes a performance, in which she is both actor and audience, "without the ability to love"'. She hides behind the characters of Carol and Willie. For Donna, the worst of the problem was that in adopting a false self, she has lost contact with her ability to feel her feelings. She says, 'I had created an ego detached from the self which was still shackled by crippled emotions'. Carol strove for social acceptance. In doing so, Donna's life became a performance: 'I could say what I thought but not what I felt. It made me a shell of a person who had created Carol in order to communicate'.

To return to Sandra, it appears that she is also looking for her lost self, her 'feeling self' in the mirror. This is far from vanity, she is not admiring herself since she has no self to be admired. Donna speaks movingly of when she was mirror watching of 'just trying to find her way back home to me'.

There is an intuition of loss – and feeling that somewhere (out there) is the image which actually reflects who she really is.

Sandra's adopted personae are distinguished by voice. Once one has heard it, there is no mistaking who is around at this particular instant. At this stage we begin to unravel the difficulty she is experiencing and see how it is that, by showing our disapproval of the Sandra who is aggressive and hurts people and paying attention and relating to the easy-to-manage-cheerful Sandra, we are reinforcing the split which underlies her behavioural problem. (The most likely start for Sandra's split is that she learned at an early stage that her negative feelings were unacceptable, so she hived them off. Alternatively, or perhaps alongside, she may be so sensitive to her feelings that they cause her more pain than she can bear. Either way, if they are not 'part of her' she does not have to take responsibility for them.) We increase the split between positive Sandra and negative Sandra if we collude with her defensive 'brain-game'. Agreeing with her that her 'bad' bit is bad, drives the wedge ever deeper between Sandra and her ability to feel.

So I am looking for a way of bringing the voices back home again, integrating them. We shall not help Sandra do this if we reject that part of her which is antisocial. We have to show her that we value all of how she feels, not just selected bits.

To some extent we already have Sandra onside. As mentioned above, when she felt she wanted to hit me she did tell herself she was not going to attack. She was trying to use what was fairly obviously a learned phrase, to control her aggression.

At lunch we take her to buy some fish and chips. Because of the narrow space, I have to stand behind her in the queue. Without knowing quite how, I can feel that she is becoming disturbed and realize that she is aware of me but cannot see what I am doing. I ask the man in front if I can stand by her side. As soon as she sees me, Sandra mutters, 'Phoebe's standing beside me now.' It is as if she is reassuring herself. It is on the way back to the day centre that I hear her muttering that she is *not* going to attack me. I was lucky to have sensed her distress, but more often she is overwhelmed by her defence response and negative feelings.

Like with Josh and Mary, I did find that even with Sandra who is fluently verbal it helped her if in addition to talking to her, I also used her body language to communicate, doing things with her which her brain recognized as part of her inner world 'language'. The time when Sandra seemed to be most engaged with her true identity was when she was kissing her arm. When I kissed mine she looked at me and laughed and said in a very relaxed and amused way, 'She's kissing her arm,' and we shared the joke. Her voice was not at all like either her false-cheerful-but-rather-stilted or her growly way of speaking. It sounded centred, like a real her.

As with a number of people with severe learning disability, some of her behaviour has been socially unacceptable. 'No' and 'Don't' are a feature of such lives. Sandra has learned to view everything she 'feels' as negative, something to be split off and hidden away. Every time we reject her negative side we are driving the wedge further in between her and how she feels herself to be. We need to try and reverse this by showing Sandra that we validate her feelings, that they do exist and are real, are not just a figment of her imagination. When Sandra says that she is or is not going to hit us, instead of saying that this is wrong, we can acknowledge that this is how she feels by saying, 'You must feel like hitting me sometimes?' This way round acknowledges that the facet of Sandra which feels angry is real and we can accept that this is real. In doing so we give her a sub-text that her feelings are part of her true identity. When I tried this, her response was to relax and say 'Yes I do', but in an almost surprised way, as if she had not really known how she felt until then and was meeting herself for the first time. So listening to the emotional content of negative communications is vital if we are to understand the landscape of our partner's world.

This switch of Sandra's voice to centredness, rather than engagement with her bright but detached voice which gave the impression that it was part of a defensive shield, brought home to me what should have been obvious. That is, the extent to which one of the effects of using Intensive Interaction to communicate is that it both addresses and speaks from the real self. There is nothing to hide behind, we reveal ourselves in our entirety, good bits and bad bits, with no pretence. It is only when we exist for each other as we are that true communication takes place. This is the place we can begin to explore each other.

Quite who a person sees in the mirror – which of their selves – can alter according to circumstances. Like Tom, whose story follows, Sandra started to see her bad side when she looked in the mirror.

Different voices

Tom is another person who has different 'learned voices' and is also fascinated by his image in the mirror. I heard four quite different personae while I was with him. The most obvious switch was to his 'telephone voice', a high-pitched social stereotypic voice, clearly derived from a woman's voice. When he is relaxed and talking about what he would like – a family and children who are quiet when they are told – he uses a quiet calm voice. He has another when he meets people, leaning too far forward and close and speaking too loudly, 'And how are you today?'

He also has a different 'voice' when he addresses himself in the mirror, when he will shout or swear at himself or use non-verbal sounds. This is where he meets his negative persona. Standing at a distance, what we need to do is join in and validate his negative sounds (and so his negative feelings) in a way that is softer but still recognizably related.

In summary, if we find people who use different voices for different occasions and who show particular interest in their mirror image, the chances are they have split off their feelings since these have always been perceived as negative. In doing so they have lost touch with how they feel. These repressed feelings can explode unexpectedly leading to outbursts of aggression. To help them we have to adopt strategies which lead towards reintegration.

As well as coping with the outside world through an adopted persona, an individual on the autistic spectrum may learn certain phrases to which they resort in social situations. The link between the brain's defensive mode and the adoption of different voices is especially clear with Patrick, who as soon as he starts to become overloaded with incoming signals switches into a loud voice with stereotypic phrases as his behaviour becomes more agitated. This happens, for example, when two people speak at once. His brain fills up with conflicting messages which he is unable to sort, so he focuses on a mode that acts as a shield: 'If I switch into my stereotypic phrases I do not have to listen to, what Donna Williams calls the unprocessed "blah-blah" from outside.'

As we shall see in the next chapter, on sensory integration, the way to disengage him from his stereotypic mode is to nudge him, that is to give him a proprioceptive stimulus, presenting him with a signal in alternative mode.

Finally, Kim Peek is the autistic savant who was the inspiration for Dustin Hoffman's character in the film *Rain Man*. Kim has a truly phenomenal memory, but a scan of his brain shows that the corpus callosum, a band of nerve fibres joining the right and left halves of the brain, is missing. Psychological testing suggests that although he is socially outgoing his actual social skills are poor. According to the 2006 television documentary, *The Real Rain Man*, he has a few pat phrases through which he has learned to deal with the world whoever he is with: characteristically, he grips the person he is with by the arms and tells them that they have become 'important people', regardless of their situation. His psychologist says that he 'never really seems to get outside of himself'.

Interestingly, Kim was unable to 'look at' people until age forty, when he became the model for the film character. Kim refers to this time as, 'when I *became* the rain man'. In other words he learned to make contact with people when he was given an identity, an alternative persona, with whom he could identify and behind whom he could shelter.

There is a difficulty here for some people on the spectrum which is largely unrecognized and which I have already touched on in the discussion of Davy using PECS, and also in the history (in *Finding You Finding Me*) of a small boy who was verbal and so accomplished on his computer – but only able to relate when I used his body language. The problem seems to be that in focusing on teaching functional communication systems such as PECS, effective as it is, we may still leave the individual isolated, able to communicate what they want but unable to break out into real interest in a world outside themselves, however their own world has enlarged. It is possible to teach someone to recognize a picture of a smile or of a sad face, but it does not help them into a position of reciprocal feeling. They remain trapped in their own affective experience, unable to explore any landscape but their own. Possibly the greatest benefit of Intensive Interaction is that it allows the partners to communicate at the level of feeling. There is genuine emotional contact in almost all exchanges.

13

Rub It Better

Because there is considerable variation in how people see the process that is known as Intensive Interaction, sometimes people seem to get the idea that they have 'done it'.

They say 'We did it for half a term' and then ask what they should do next. In this chapter we are going to explore the idea that using Intensive Interaction is an ongoing engagement that can be used by anyone who wants to get close to their partner. So it can be of help to anyone who is involved in care in whatever capacity.

To look at how this works out, this chapter takes the form of a conversation between myself (Phoebe) and Jane Horwood, who is a paediatric occupational therapist using the technique known as 'Sensory Integration' with children and adults with a range of developmental difficulties. First of all we are going to take a look at what is meant by Sensory Integration, and then we shall move on to how using body language has helped in its practice, particularly through a case study of Harriet, a small girl with very severe autism and acute hypersensitivities.

Recently Jane attended a workshop on Intensive Interaction and is finding that this adds to the quality of the service she can offer. My particular interest in touch stems from observations that whereas a child or adult may not respond directly to my using their sounds to respond to them, if I place these alongside movements that are also part of their repertoire, they start to attend. It is as if the rhythms of sound are 'hard-wired in' and make sense to them, where the sounds alone do not get through. It is partly that I am switching modes of presentation in order to catch attention, but it also seems that for many people on the autistic spectrum, the tactile and proprioceptive senses continue to carry meaning when the others have broken up. We have met two examples of this, when Alex was able to cross the road if he was carrying full shopping bags and Davy could walk straight in from the garden if he was holding his play-dough pot full of dough. Previously, without the weight to feel, these boys lay down wherever they were when they lost a coherent sense of what they were doing and could no longer orientate themselves.

Before going on to asking how the use of Intensive Interaction might help a practitioner in another discipline, my first observation to Jane is that I think we should both agree that in a world which is no longer making sense, our task is to find ways of focusing our partner's attention on some person, activity or object which has significance for our partner.

Jane: Yes. When I am working with any individual I have to try and find what is meaningful for them. From a sensory integration point of view, we depend on the sensory information we receive from our environment to make sense of what is going on round us. If such information is confusing and uncomfortable, we may depend on a very specific sensation, such as touch or tactile input, to try and provide a meaningful stimulus the brain can understand, and even use this to block out sensations that are painful, confusing and distressing.

Phoebe: So when, for example, an autistic person's processing system gets 'stuck' in one mode (when their brain has lost the capacity to form a coherent picture of their environment from the sensory input they are receiving), it is sometimes possible to bypass this blockage by using an alternative sensory route. Donna Williams spells this out in her new book, *The Jumbled Jigsaw*, when she is talking about 'information processing delay'. She says that she found it helped her to process what she was seeing if she could tap or move it – the acoustics or nature of the movement gave her a better sense of the object's nature, from which she could derive its meaning. In order to process the nature of the object, she needed to supplement her visual sense with an auditory or tactile input.

Jane: In addition, from a sensory interaction point of view, if we tap an object, we get a vibration through our arm. If we tap it firmly enough, we can even jar our joints. These sensory inputs can help to calm an over-responsive tactile system by providing additional proprioceptive input.

Phoebe: To change direction a little, I find touch quite difficult to think about, partly because we do not always make the distinction between the active and the passive mode, you touch me – I feel you. And the object of our feeling is sensed in so many ways, shape, texture, weight, temperature.

Jane: Touch is still a sense that we do not fully understand, but one that is important to all of us. It is the first to develop in the womb and our largest sensory system. It is very complex. Tactile impulses that tell us about touch, pressure, texture, cold, heat and pain seem to go just about everywhere in the brain – without a sense of touch there appears to be a poorly balanced nervous system. Apart from the tactile sensations there is also proprioception, inputs into the body that require muscle stretching and contracting and joint input. For example, carrying a heavy bag provides not only a tactile stimulation – I feel the handle in my hands – but also a proprioceptive sensation in the body. So the two systems, tactile and proprioception, work closely together and are integrated via a common pathway in the brain. Sometimes this joint information is referred to as 'somatosense'. For example, when I brush a child's arm in a particular way, I am working hard to desensitize their overprotective tactile responses, but when I encourage a child to wear a weighted pack at playtime, I am working to actively engage the proprioceptive system through heavy work.

Phoebe: Then is it that light touch sets off the tactile sensors which are difficult to process whereas firm touch sets off the proprioceptive sensors which are easier to process? Is this why there is a different response?

Jane: As a hypothesis based on observations of children within my clinical settings, I suggest that it is probably easier to think of how the brain processes exactly where that touch has occurred. If touch is firm and maintained for approximately six seconds, then the combination of the tactile and proprioceptive receptors *aids* the processing, partly by the modulating influence of the proprioceptive system. Light touch is much more difficult to localize. Initially it is alerting and stimulating but, if it is fleeting, then the brain may be bombarded with other stimuli and unable to filter what has just happened.

Heavy muscle work such as pulling, pushing, carrying, lifting and tugging is often used by clinicians to prepare an individual for a tactile experience. For example, a parent might be encouraged to apply deep massage to a child's gums before eating. So a child who knocks themselves and is told to 'rub it better' is being given advice based on a sound premise: deep pressure helps to counter the sensitivity triggered by light touch.

John can't cope with light touch, especially people brushing past him in the playground. So he pushes them over or hits out. But when he does this, he receives a wonderful jarring sensation in his joints. This 'avoiding light touch' and initiating hard work in his joints and muscles is a proprioceptive stimulus that helps him to cope in the playground. John is given a backpack with a heavy book in it to wear and encouraged to take part in activities involving pushing, pulling, carrying and lifting. Within a week he has become sufficiently tolerant of touch so that he can even stand in line, an activity which involves a lot of light touch.

Although people with autism may have difficulty in determining if a sensation is threatening, most of us do not, but we may have difficulty in knowing exactly where the touch has occurred and its shape. For example, if someone draws a letter on your back, it is sometimes difficult to convert the sensation into a real letter, perhaps because the location of the touch has been difficult. Many people who have had a limb amputated report tactile sensations from a limb that no longer exists.

Phoebe: Perhaps this relates to some recent research, that when we 'locate' touch in our arm, there is also an 'image' in our brain of where it is, and that it is possible to trick the arm into thinking it is being touched when it is not. What is more extraordinary is that, under experimental conditions, the brain representation fires when it 'thinks' that the arm has been touched, even though this is an illusion (Blankenburg *et al.* 2006).

To return to Sensory Integration, I understand that this approach was introduced by Dr Jean Ayres in the 1950s (Ayres 1972, 2005). So could you tell me what it aims to do and how you go about it?

Jane: Sensory Integration is the organization of all the endless pieces of sensory information which enter the brain during the day so that they do not just remain as individual bits and that the brain can use them. For example, the brain has to locate where the information is coming from, to sort and organize that information in order to allow the body to move, learn, behave and interact successfully. Of course it is not just touch that needs integration, all the sensory systems are involved, no single system works on its own without influencing the others. When the endless flow of information is, for whatever reason, perceived as confusing or threatening, the brain is seemingly stuck in a rush-hour traffic jam. If you have a major problem in your vestibular system (gravity perception), it is highly likely you will also have difficulties with your tactile/touch system. In order to pinpoint a dysfunction there has to be a basic understanding of the development of sensory integration in the infant's brain. For example, while a baby with sound tactile sensory integration development will find it calming and emotionally satisfying to be held in their mother's arms, in an infant on the autistic spectrum this same stimulus may be somehow processed as threatening. Their normal protective tactile responses over-react, so they may arch their backs and squirm away when cuddled, crying out in pain. They still desire to be comforted by their mothers through touch, but the reality is that their tactile system is telling their brain this is uncomfortable and painful. This is known as 'tactile defensiveness' and originates in a protective function. As well as this, touch allows us to discriminate, for example, through the weight and feel of a fabric. A child with tactile defensiveness is upset and confused by certain tactile sensations, so may try to avoid them by hiding under a table or refusing to wear certain garments. They may become distressed by hair brushing, nail cutting and, as we saw when we talked about Bill, by the sensory impact of showers.

Like Intensive Interaction, studies on baby monkeys deprived of touch indicate that comfortable touch sensation is an essential part of the formation of attachment between mother and baby. Both approaches are working with systems that have their roots in early development. Particularly, the effectiveness of deep touch in bringing meaning to an overloaded system may relate to the sensation experienced by the growing foetus surrounded by fluid within a muscular womb.

Phoebe: So when you have, more or less, isolated whereabouts in the sensory system there is a deficit, do you then set to work trying to repair this (in the hope of retraining the brain or setting up alternative neurone pathways) or do you, as in Intensive Interaction, look for some stimulus the brain already shows signs of understanding and feeling comfy with and work from that? In fact, how do you, in a therapeutic sense, go about integration?

Jane: The 'specialness' of Sensory Integration is that, like Intensive Interaction, it is based on observable evidence. In addition to specific standardized tests, time is taken to watch the child at home and school and observe which ways they use or avoid tactile input. This information is used to see where alternative inputs may be helpful. Light pressure is often experienced by an overloaded system as painful, so the therapist will use the deep pressure or weight that is reassuring. This may need to be in specific places. For example, a man with fragile X syndrome, who only tolerated pressure on his hands, shoulders and feet, relaxed completely when pressure was applied in the region of the hips. On the other hand, a child with foetal alcohol syndrome, who presented as having ADHD (attention deficit hyperactivity disorder), was completely calm squashed under a weighted blanket. A young girl likes to wear underwear she has outgrown and pyjamas too small for her. The pressure of these tight garments helped her to feel all right in her world. If a child is very young, Sensory Integration Therapy can actually assist the growth of new neural connections. Depending on the level of disability, interventions can allow the brain to make sense of the information coming in, to inhibit some messages and pay attention to others. In the long term, there may need to be the provision of a 'sensory diet', for example, foot massage before going to bed, blankets and sheets tucked in tightly instead of duvets on the bed, weighted back-packs at playtime and games involving tactile stimulation, such as 'lucky dips' in rice or dry pasta. Jean Ayres encourages us to tap into the child's innate desire to play. Martin has a history of aggressive behaviour. I engage him in heavy muscle work, swinging, throwing, jumping, crashing. He then starts to stroke my hair and manoeuvre himself onto my lap for a cuddle.

Phoebe: So can we turn now to your work with Harriet, a small girl whose severe autism is characterized by auditory and visual hypersensitivity (she cannot cope with certain sounds and prefers dim light), she does not like certain textures, she is under-reactive to pain and temperature and to certain movements (she does not get dizzy when spinning). She easily becomes overwhelmed by too much sensory input. You say that in order to stay within her 'sensory comfort zone' she flits from one activity to another, resisting interaction because of the demands it makes of her. She cannot filter out irrelevant sensory information. This is exhausting and emotionally draining and does not leave much energy for learning. Consequently, she tries to control her environment and can appear stubborn. She is in a constant state of high anxiety. I gather that your work with her involves a variety of weight and tactile sensory programmes, and that it is already accompanied by substantial benefit. Could you tell me in what sense, how it has made it easier to use Intensive Interaction as well as Sensory Integration?

Jane: Harriet loves to be squeezed and squashed by her parents and especially to have her feet massaged – but when I started to try and work with her, she was reluctant to let me sit near her, let alone touch her. After I came to the workshop on Intensive Interaction, I tried tuning in to her rhythms. While she sat on an inflatable mattress, I bounced her, as she said 'wibble-wobble, wibble-wobble'. As she relaxed I was able to apply deep pressure to her legs and feet, resulting in an enormous grin and verbal request for wibble wobble. We have progressed to a variety of tactile and proprioceptive inputs, which now make it possible for Harriet to hold hands and sit near people. It is also helping with her noise sensitivity.

Phoebe: I need to interrupt here with an observation by Donna Williams again. She said on a Channel 4 television programme, *Jam Jar*, broadcast in 1995, that when she wears coloured lenses, which cut down her visual overload, she can hear better. It is almost as if we have a finite processing capacity. If we cut down on one input, we leave space for another.

Jane: Using Intensive Interaction alongside Sensory Integration has speeded up the process of being able to work with Sensory Integration. I get a quicker response. For example, by session three, Harriet was able to sit with her mother on a swing and throw beanbags into a bucket. (Previously she would not have allowed anyone to sit on the swing with her, let alone engage in a purposeful activity.) My normal experience of working with autistic children is that it takes at least four sessions even to begin to engage in meaningful activity. Harriet was so keen last time she came that she made it clear that she wanted to play before she got her coat off.

Phoebe: So when you are using Intensive Interaction, what you are doing is using Harriet's body language to make contact with her so that you can more easily proceed with helping her deal with her sensory distress?

Jane: It helps me to re-establish contact quickly with children whom I only see intermittently and also enables me to reach children who, although they may have previously accepted sessions of sensory integration, have done so passively. For example, Adam is a large adolescent boy on the autistic spectrum. He is deeply withdrawn into his world, interested in picking up and eating the tiniest bits of fluff he sees on the floor. He constantly flicks his fingers in front of his face. Progress has been slow, and at the end of each session I was left feeling I had not really made contact with him. After his last therapy session, I met him in the school soft play area. When he bent to pick up a piece of fluff, I did so also. Before it reached his mouth, he stopped to look at me. I placed my pretend bit of fluff in my pocket. He smiled, and extended his hand, offering me his piece also. I squeezed his hand, applying firm pressure and then took his piece and placed it in my pocket. Throughout this exchange Adam kept eye-contact, and his facial expression appeared to say, 'At last we can start communicating.' He came out of his extreme passive state and started actively to interact. I used different fabrics to rub his arm to stimulate his tactile system and encouraged him to choose his source of sensation. It was the most interactive session we have had so far.

I am also exploring using Intensive Interaction with more able individuals and finding it helps with those who are anxious and acting out. These children are often astonished and stop in their tracks at this mad lady who is thumping the equipment as they are or extending their rather interesting speech patterns. I shall continue to explore. But coming back to Harriet, I think Intensive Interaction has given us both a foundation we can work from. It is more easy to offer her a framework of sensory communications now that we can communicate, and Harriet now has ways of letting me know when I get her needs wrong. The other day she was flitting and would not attend no matter how I tried to intervene. When she arrived at the inflatable mattress she said 'wibble-wobble'. I immediately started to engage her through her rhythms, and the rest of the session went from strength to strength. I feel that now we both have 'ownership' of Intensive Interaction and can choose to use the technique to engage or re-engage appropriately.

Phoebe: Like you, I find Intensive Interaction involves me in an ongoing learning situation. Each person is different and amazingly responsive once we get the language right.

At this point Harriet's mother, Margaret, and her teacher, Clare, wanted to add how the joint intervention had affected their ability to relate and work and play with Harriet.

Margaret: When Jane added Intensive Interaction to Sensory Integration there was an immediate change in Harriet's response. She became much more tolerant of Jane being physically close and would even allow Jane to touch her! Harriet vocalized much more and used several new words. 'Brilliant!' was one such exclamation which we had never heard Harriet say before. Harriet's enjoyment of the sessions seemed to increase, and she changed from wanting to do things on her terms to being more cooperative. This switch happened more quickly with each session.

The only time Harriet responded negatively to the Intensive Interaction was during a session which, for the first time, involved her brother. The two banged heads at one point by accident, and for a few minutes afterwards Harriet was cross and responded angrily to Jane's attempts at using her language. Fortunately, this was only short lived and Harriet was brought back on task within a few minutes.

One piece of equipment which Harriet particularly enjoyed was a large inflatable cushion. Harriet loved to lie on this whilst Jane pushed the cushion causing Harriet's body and head to jolt up and down. Jane altered the rhythm of the movement making it quicker, and amazingly Harriet speeded up her babble to keep up with the timing. As Jane slowed down, so did Harriet. It became a game which Harriet was clearly enjoying!

Harriet has been described by her class teacher as a 'sponge for Intensive Interaction'. However, with major sensory issues, the simultaneous use of the two interventions (Sensory Integration plus Intensive Interaction) with Harriet has demonstrated a rapid improvement in her tolerance levels. Since embarking on this programme Harriet seems to have turned a corner, and one of Harriet's teaching assistants has described her as a 'different child'. Long may this continue!

And finally, this is what Harriet's teacher has to say.

Clare: Prior to this academic year, I had used Intensive Interaction approaches with individual children and found it immensely successful for both building relationships and developing early communication, including speech. However, this year I was faced with a very different class, most of whom had severe learning difficulties combined with autistic spectrum conditions, so I decided to use it with all the pupils as part of our day-to-day work, encouraging support staff to do the same.

During the summer holidays, I made a home visit to Harriet's family. I was in the home for more than an hour, during which time I was completely ignored by Harriet. While not unduly concerned by this, I felt it essential to build bridges between us as quickly as possible, in order for Harriet to make progress in school. From her first day in my class, I began using her body language when she would tolerate it. Within the first week, we had developed a complex turn-taking game based on finger movements, and by the end of the week I received my first 'bear hug' from

Harriet. We had the beginnings of a warm relationship, which we have been able to build on since.

At the beginning of the year Harriet had a fondness for two particular members of support staff – Michele (a teaching assistant) and Nikki (lunchtime supervisor and part-time teaching assistant). I noticed that their interactions with her included elements of an Intensive Interaction approach. For example, Nikki used a favourite song at lunchtime to get Harriet to wash her hands, always ending in a strong hug. Michele would often calm Harriet when upset by using calming sounds based on Harriet's own. Both were confident in touching Harriet, always using firm pressure.

Harriet seemed erratic in terms of her levels of cooperation. Some days she would sit on a chair at a table to do her work. Other days she would climb on the adult working with her, or crawl under the table. She might throw her work or try to stand on the table. Sometimes she would refuse to go to the table at all. Adults were often smacked in the face. She sometimes responded well to rewards, using 'First work, then… [reward]', but on other days would scream at this approach. We found that Intensive Interaction could often enable Harriet to attempt some work. For example, if she wanted to lie on the floor, I would lie beside her. If Harriet made sounds, I would either join in with them, or tap their rhythm on the floor. If she made body movements, I would echo and adapt them. This would often develop into a turn-taking game and eventually ended with Harriet climbing onto me or hugging me for physical contact. Harriet was more likely then to do some of her work, particularly if it was brought over to her. Other staff who worked with Harriet also worked with her in this way.

This is where we were before Harriet began her Sensory Integration therapy. Since then, we have seen considerable progress in terms of concentration, cooperation and contentment. She is slower to become frustrated, often giving us time to prevent distress occurring at all. She is much more tolerant of the noise made by other pupils. It is easier and quicker to calm her when she is upset or cross. I sit or lie on the floor near her, and she allows (or asks for with gesture) firm pressure on her legs and feet. We take Harriet's work to her now, allowing her to do it in whichever position suits her at the time. This can involve her lying over an adult on her tummy to do drawing work or bouncing on the trampette while she is being read to. Sometimes she chooses to be in a room with no other children or in the darkened bathroom. Harriet still does not always want to do her work, but no longer throws it or hits the adult she is with. It is not a case of her doing it on her 'own terms' but of doing it under the appropriate sensory conditions that help her to concentrate.

I just want to stop here and emphasize the need to respect what we might see as unusual or even odd behaviour. When Harriet is bouncing she has a focus which helps her cut out distractions so she can actually hear the story being read to her. When she is lying over her teacher, again, the pressure of physical contact makes it possible for her to concentrate her mind on the task in hand. It is absolutely no good trying to force a child into a position where they are at the mercy of their scrambled brain, where they have nothing to cling on to.

Therapist, teacher, mother and all Harriet's support workers have joined together and work closely to help Harriet. Although Harriet still experiences sensory hypersensitivities, respecting the difficulties these cause her and using her body language has offered a vehicle to carry all their other skills. They can now keep her attention both in class and during the Sensory Integration therapy sessions which are helping her to compensate for her processing difficulties. At home she is much more manageable and affectionate.

14

What Next?

I live in the country. A friend was looking after some sheep while the shepherd was away. When he needed to move the sheep from one field to the next he made a gap, moving the temporary wire fence in such a way as to leave an overlap. When the shepherd returned, my friend asked him why the sheep would not go through the gap but remained in their original field. The old man replied that he needed to get down on his knees and look at it from the sheep's point of view. Then he would see...

This minor pastoral anecdote is a perfect illustration of how we fail to see the world from any point of view other than our own – and how, if we are to make effective engagement, we need to leave our sense of what is our own reality behind and enter the sensory perceptive field of those who we are trying to engage.

So what have we learned from the people we have met so far, people who – whether or not they were on the autistic spectrum – can only be described as living isolated and unfulfilled lives?

The journey from isolation to intimacy can only be accomplished through trust, so that we can move from a position of aloneness to one of total acceptance. We have to move away from the idea of 'caring' to one of partnership, so that our partner no longer feels himself or herself to be an object to whom life happens as a kaleidoscope of barely related events which they survive as best they can, but a valued individual whose feelings and needs are sought out and treasured.

One of the commonest failures of care at present is that we come into work, we do everything we are asked, but we never actually reach out beyond ourselves to engage with our partner. This is very often a failure of imagination and training rather than intent. The outcome for would-be partners is just as disastrous, leaving them in an emotional wasteland. When I had shown them how to get in touch with their partner, a support worker said, 'I see that doing is not enough, I have to be there for them.'

In practical terms, the key to building trust is engagement with how our partner feels. One of the questions each of us has to ask ourselves, is whether we are willing to put our own life patterns on hold in favour of reaching out (beyond our own experiences) to those of our partner, in a way that has meaning for them, one which says, 'I am here for you, you are not alone.' We do this, not so much through a leap into the dark but by placing ourselves in their sensory perceptive world.

First we have to find a common language, so that we can show our partners we are listening to and responding to how they feel. Our interest and engagement must be demonstrable (physically within their field of vision or hearing – and in such a mode that it does not require elaborate interpretation) so that our partners can grasp our intent. And secondly, we have to use our heightened sensitivity to enter their world and see it from their point of view.

If we look back through the eyes of the people we have met in this book, we see that each has a unique personal story; our job is to try and see life as they see it. For example, we have to attend not only to their physical disabilities, such as lack of vision, hearing and mobility, but also to those sensory experiences to which they may be hypersensitive and reduce these.

We need to understand why a person functions in a particular way. If we look through Hannah's sensory experience (remembering she has no sight) we have to think about what it is she is hearing. With Bill, we needed to look at how his accommodation was planned and rearrange the way it was used in order to reduce the stress to which its misuse subjected him. And then why can't Alex cross the road to see his Auntie? Can we give him a better sense of what he is doing by providing a stimulus that his brain can recognize and use to maintain a sense of coherence? Why is Davy able to spell his name on the wall (vertical as on TV) rather than on the table (horizontal)? Why does Rosie lie on the floor with her back to the wall and what does this tell us about her life in the past? Why does Niall sit in the corner of the room under his bed with a pillow over his ears? (Both Rosie and Niall are in retreat but not for the same reason.) We need to grasp the logic of what people are doing, their logic not ours.

And we must learn to listen to our partners in every sense of the word. It is no good our trying to force them into the patterns of our reality. This has been tried and has not worked for them: in spite of all our best efforts they are still on their own. But as soon as we start to listen to their body language, we find we are able to communicate with each other. Learning to tap into the way they talk to themselves, their personal language, gives us access to how they feel and brings us to engagement with each other. We need to open ourselves, to accept what is 'not self' in an attitude of trust and love.

But in engaging in this conversational relationship, there are other aspects of their lives to which we must pay attention. It goes without saying that we need to look at their physical welfare – and yet people with cerebral palsy may still be badly seated, and deafness is overlooked because it is assumed that their inability to connect is part of their learning disability.

When children and adults with autism are difficult to look after because their behaviour is self-injurious or aggressive, it is still assumed that somehow the fault lies in them, that they are difficult, manipulative and even dangerous – and that this can somehow be controlled by programmes of behavioural modification, extra staff and restraint, instead of regarding their outburst as primarily a response to stress which has its roots in painful external or internal sensations.

Fear is at the root of so much aggression: fear of physical assault based on previous if not current experience (Jenny) and fear of being pushed into painful fragmentation by sensory overload in those on the autistic spectrum (Pranve, Stan, Bill and Nick, for example). In order to protect itself, the body triggers its defences to respond to perceived attack.

So as well learning the language we need to look at the triggers for an outburst, such as Bill's need for a calm area when he enters his house – and understand why he cannot bear showers because the needle streams of hot water are intolerably painful. The problem is a logistic one and not an extra. We have to meet these needs by rearranging living space if necessary. We must understand that if we do not give weight to his problems, we are responsible for his distress. Hiring more care staff will not resolve his outbursts. We must find the causes.

On the whole we are aware of the need to try and let people know what is happening, but we do not always frame our timetables or communications in language that has meaning for them. We may be unaware of the limitations of their visual or auditory field. In some cases we may push the acquisition of our language too hard, so that its use becomes misdirected (Mary) or used as a barrier rather than a point of access (Sandra).

However, one of the most astonishing aspects of using language based on our partner's own sounds and movements is that their brain finds this mode of interaction so powerful that it can override the pain and confusion resulting from overloading stimuli, triggers that can otherwise lead to violence. A possible explanation lies in the recent suggestion that all 'intimate conversations' produce oxytocin, the 'feel-good' hormone which boosts trust by reducing the activity of the amygdala (our red-alert system). Alongside this, our partner's brain is being offered external markers that it can focus on to the exclusion of its internal chaos. This is particularly evident when the external marker is offered in a sense that has not fragmented; for example when we use touch and weights and deep massage a child who has extreme sensitivity to light and sounds.

Does it matter to us that some of our most precious human attributes, such as trust, are being reduced to biochemistry? Why does this feel as if it is to deny their value? Like it or not, we are going to have to get used to the idea of the intimate company of neurotransmitters. But before we feel we are being shrunk out of existence, perhaps we should remember that these are the executive, rather than the director. There is still someone around who can ask, who is this person who feels great or miserable or whatever, who is observer number one? Whoever is in charge, if we let go of ourselves we find we can come to a stage where communication takes off, flying free like Jack and his partner roller-blading into a single purpose, liberating us both.

Referring to the use of their body language with people on the autistic spectrum, Rowan Williams (2005) points out that the process involves, 'intensified listening'. The language we use with each other is, he says, 'not just a matter of finding a mutually acceptable way of talking, allowing the unsaid to be said; it is also a teasing out of what is said in new directions by a listening that seeks to pick up the rhythms of another's communication'.

The question is, what are we listening to, in fact what can we possibly be listening to since our partners cannot use words? What do we mean by language in this sense? To return to Rowan Williams: 'Where communication is broken, dysfunctional, turned back on itself, persons are trapped; care for persons is care for their language, listening to the worlds they inhabit'. The only thing we can hear in this sense is how they feel – and however it works, our body language is the voice of the limbic system, how we feel. If we want truly to get to know each other, we may have to abandon the cognitive scaffolding of words and look to body language to open the doors to affective relationship. Total and intimate attention to our partner not only leads to understanding but opens us out to the depths of their perspective, we begin to see the world from our partner's standpoint. To go back to a practitioner who is feeling her way into the possibilities and meaning of real communication:

> Stepping into someone else's world teaches us about ourselves as well as about them and reaching further into our own world and meanings and existence provides us with deeper contemplations of what meanings and existences might be for others. To truly know another person and truly be open to who they are, we must first know and be open to ourselves…a progressive relationship between two communication partners where barriers of power, superiority-inferiority/normal-abnormal are non-existent and where learning about oneself and others and connecting are central. (Michelle O'Neill, personal communication)

Intimacy seems to demand a culmination. Regardless of the nature of their disability (even if my partner is deeply autistic) and however isolated they have been, almost all the videoed material I have of interactions – and the majority of unvideoed sessions, reach a point of deep intimacy, either that of prolonged gaze or a physical hug. Such gestures normally seem as if they are accompanied by a feeling of enormous relief. This is the place where we feel totally at home with each other.

At the same time, our lives consist of process rather than stasis. However enjoyable the peaks may be, we cannot live on summits but have to come down. So is there an après-ski, an after-closeness? It does appear that the effects of using body language spread outside the interactional sessions and relationships improve in a general fashion.

And yet to ask 'What next?' is to mistake the nature of Intensive Interaction. In itself it is not an end but a means, a way that can be used progressively to open out our lives and enrich them. As we become more sensitive to our partner's body language it becomes easier to read the clues and interpret distress signals whether they be short-term contingent responses, such as muscles tensing, the alteration of posture, the flinch, the flicker of an eyelid, or long-term defences, the different voices that echo the false persona adopted to disguise vulnerability. We become more aware of the sometimes subtle distinctions between fixation and enjoyment. We literally begin to sense the world from their sensory point of view. This becomes more than just monitoring; it is as if, by immersing ourselves in their world, we feel in ourselves their perception of personal space, move with them close to or away from a person or source of stimulus.

We might call this 'insight', but this still implies that we are outside and suddenly transported to a view of what is going on inside our partner. The condition I am trying to find words to describe here should perhaps more accurately be seen as 'insidesight'. Maybe in the end, through sharing the sensory experience of our partners, we simply become transparent to their sensory world.

Transparent but not lost. We still need to keep a sharp eye on the path leading back, making use of the cognitive processes of our brain, particularly the respectful consideration of what we have learned. We no longer see behaviour of our partners through our perspective of the need to control it, but can use our in-depth understanding of their world to rethink and modify their environment so that it becomes user-friendly. This dyadic exchange is that of coming together, of interchange and emerging transformed. From this close intimacy we become part of each other's world. We begin to see, not just the fact of Jim scratching the wall but, looking out from our shared sensory experience, the feel of *why* he is doing it. 'I feel it in my bones.'

Part of the intention of this book was to ask if there was anything else we needed to do as well as to learn our partner's body language – an outsider's view of how else we needed to change our partner's world. Exploration of this idea led to the somewhat unexpected conclusion that in the practice of Intensive Interaction it is not only our partner's behaviour that is changed, we are also changed. In our heightened sensitivity we have come together, no longer experiencing separate lives but moving from witness to participant, true partners with a common reality. A more skilled reading of subliminal clues leads us to shared perspective. It is from this inner platform that we can effect helpful changes to their environment and reduce the events which are causing them distress.

Our attitude, the language we share, our partner's physical well-being and responses to their environment, are these all part of Intensive Interaction?

Because it works so fluently, people will sometimes say that it is intuitive in a way that suggests there is something almost magical about it. This is unhelpful. Rather, we should think of it as a tool which enables us to walk the tricky but liberating path between insight and cognition, one that helps us to develop sensitivity to the sensory reality experienced by our partner. I have to go back to the idea that it is a journey rather than a destination, a journey on which we take not just our tickets but all the sensory baggage as well.

Although he cannot speak, the last word should be with Davy (who we met on page 116). Davy is the small boy who has very severe autism. He is extremely hypersensitive with major behavioural outbursts. He actualizes his inner world through models and drawings. I had introduced his teachers to the technique of using body language with him a few months previously. One day he starts to make a necklace out of his construction kit. His teacher makes an identical one. Davy adds some more bits and his teacher copies him, then adds an extra piece. He looks at this and, rooting in his box, finds and adds the same bit to his. This continues for some time. She copies him, he copies her. He leans forward and adjusts a piece of hers that has slipped so that, like his, it is symmetrical. The next day he plays the same game with another teacher. So far one might think that he was using his partners to pursue his fixation. However, the next day, when he and his teacher have both finished their respective necklaces and *while they are still wearing their own*, he dives into his box again, produces a few more pieces and very carefully joins the two of them together. He is laughing, his face is radiant. Davy, who has no words and who is so cut off and isolated, has found a language to express his emotional transition from 'me' to 'her' to 'us together' – and shows this to his teacher in a way that leaves one gasping at his ingenuity. *'Listen to me and I will find you.'*

Above all we have to engage with the centre of the person: we need to ease our way into who they are, rather than what they do, so that they begin to get a feeling of their own worth. *'I am a person who matters to someone else.'*

Each story in this book is unfinished business: the people we have met, those who care for them, mine. We are all capable of change and need to keep ourselves open and responsive to unfolding possibilities. What I hope to have shown is that however deeply they have retreated, when we learn to use our partner's body language they will respond with generosity and pleasure.

References

Astafiev, S.V., Stanley, C.M., Shulman, G.L. and Corbetta, M. (2004) 'Extra-striate body area in human occipital cortex responds to the performance of motor actions.' Nature Reviews, *Neuroscience 7*, 542–548.

Astell, J.A. and Ellis, M.P. (2006) 'The social function of imitation in severe dementia.' *Infant and Child Development 15*, 311–319.

Ayres, A.J. (1972) *Sensory Integration and Learning Disorders.* Los Angeles: Western Psychological Services.

Ayres, A.J. (2005) *Sensory Integration and the Child.* Revised and updated by Paediatric Therapy Network Psychological Services. Los Angeles: Western Psychological Services.

Barber, M. (2006) 'Intensive Interaction: Some practical considerations.' *PMLD-Link 17*, 3, 22–27.

Baron-Cohen, S., Leslie, A.M. and Frith, U. (1985). 'Does the autistic child have a theory of mind?' *Cognition 21*, 37–46.

Barron, S. and Barron, J. (1992) *There's a Boy in Here.* New York: Simon and Schuster.

Bennett, L. (1998) 'Making sense of violent behaviour.' *The SLD Experience 22*.

Blankenburg, F., Ruff, C.C., Deichmann, R., Rees, G. and Driver, J. (2006) 'The cutaneous rabbit illusion affects human primary sensory cortex somatotropically.' *PLoS (Public Library of Science) Biology 4*, e69.

Buhusi, C.V. and Meck, W.H. (2005) 'What makes us tick? Functional and neural mechanisms of interval timing.' Nature Reviews, *Neuroscience 6*, 755–765.

Caldwell, P., and Stevens, P. (1998) *Person to Person.* Brighton: Pavilion Publishing.

Caldwell, P. with Hoghton, M. (2000) *You Don't Know What It's Like.* Brighton: Pavilion Publishing.

Caldwell, P. (2002a) *Crossing the Minefield.* Brighton: Pavilion Publishing.

Caldwell, P. (2002b) *Learning the Language* (training video). Brighton: Pavilion Publishing.

Caldwell, P. and Stevens, P. (2005) *Creative Conversations* (training video). Brighton: Pavilion Publishing.

Caldwell, P. (2006a) *Finding You Finding Me.* London: Jessica Kingsley Publishers.

Caldwell, P. (2006b) 'Speaking the other's language: Imitation as a gateway to relationship.' *Infant and Child Development 15*, 3, 275–282.

Coia, P. (2006) '*Intensive Interaction* as a therapeutic psychological intervention?' Presentation at *Intensive Interaction Conference 2006: Supporting Sustainable Innovation in Practice.* Hilton Leeds City.

Cronin, V. (1969) *The Flowering of the Renaissance.* London: Collins.

Crystal, D. (2005) *How Language Works.* Harmondsworth: Penguin Books.

Dapretto, M., Davies, M., Pfeifer, J., Scott, A., Sigman, M., Bookheimer, S. and Jacoboni, M. (2006) 'Understanding emotions in others: Mirror neuron dysfunction in children with autism spectrum disorders.' Nature Reviews, *Neuroscience 9*, 28–30.

Dawson, G. and Adams, A. (1984) 'Imitation and social responsiveness in autistic children.' *Journal of Abnormal Child Psychology 12*, 209–226.

Dawson, G. and Galpert, L. (1990) 'Mothers' use of imitative play for facilitating social responsiveness and toy play in young autistic children.' *Development and Psychopathology 2*, 151–162.

Ephraim, G.W. (1986) *A Brief Introduction to Augmented Mothering.* Playtrack Pamphlet. Radlett, Herts: Harpebury Hospital.

Escalona, A., Field, T., Nadel, J. and Lundy, B. (2000) 'Brief report: Imitation effects on children with autism.' *Journal of Autism and Developmental Disorders 32*, 2, 141–144.

Falck-Ytter, T., Gredeback, G. and von Hofsten, C. (2006) 'Infants predict other people's action goals.' Nature Reviews, *Neuroscience 9*, 878–879.

Field, T., Field, T., Sanders, C. and Nadel, J. (2001) 'Children with autism display more social behaviors after repeated imitation sessions.' *Autism 5*, 3, 317–323.

Fraiberg, S. (1977) *Insights from the Blind: Comparative Studies of Blind and Sighted Infants.* New York: Basic Books.

Gerland, G. (1996) *A Real Person.* London: Souvenir Press.

Gillingham, G. (1995) *Autism – Handle with Care.* Edmonton, Alberta: Tacit Publishing.

Goleman, D.P. (1996) *Emotional Intelligence.* London: Bloomsbury Publishing.

Grandin, T. (1992) *A is for Autism.* Film. Fine Take Productions and Channel 4 Television Corporation.

Grandin, T. and Scariano, M. (1986) *Emergence: Labelled Autistic.* New York: Warner Books.

Hamilton, J.A., Haier, R.J. and Buchsbaum, M.S. (1984) 'Intrinsic enjoyment and boredom coping scales: Validation with personality, evoked potential and attention measures.' *Personality and Individual Differences 5*, 2, 183–193.

Hart, P. (2003) 'The role of a partner in communication episodes with a deaf-blind person.' *Deafblind Review,* January–June, 4–7.

Heimann, M., Laberg, K.E. and Nordøen, B. (2006) 'Imitative interaction increases social interest and elicited imitation in non-verbal children with autism.' *Infant and Child Development 15*, 3, 297–309.

Hobson, R.P. and Lee, A. (1999) 'Imitation and identification in autism.' *Journal of Child Psychology and Psychiatry 40*, 4, 649–659.

Hollander, E., Novotny, S., Hanratty, M., Yaffe, R. *et al.* (2003) 'Oxytocin infusion reduces repetitive behaviors in adults with autistic and Asperger's disorders.' *Neuropsychopharmacology 28*, 1, 193–198.

Jolliffe, T., Lansdown, R. and Robinson, C. (1992) 'Autism: A personal account.' *Communication 26*, 3, 12–19.

Jonsson, C., Clinton, D., Fahrman, M., Mazzaglia, G., Novak, S. and Sorhus, K. (2001) 'How do mothers signal shared feeling-states to their infants? An investigation of affective attunement and imitation during the first year of life.' *Scandinavian Journal of Psychology 42*, 377–381.

Karpf, A. (2006) *The Human Voice: The Story of a Remarkable Talent.* London: Bloomsbury Publishing.

Keagan, R. (1982) *The Evolving Self.* Cambridge, MA: Harvard University Press.

Leaning, B. and Watson, T. (2006) 'From the inside looking out – an Intensive Interaction group of people with profound and multiple learning disabilities.' *British Journal of Learning Disabilities 34*, 103–109.

Mayer-Lindberg, A. (2006) Quoted in *New Scientist,* 29 April. National Institute of Mental Health.

Miles, B. (1999) *Talking the Language of the Hands to the Hands.* Monmouth, OR: DB-Link.

Nadel, J., Croue, S., Kervella, C., Mattlinger, M-J., Canet, P., Hudelot, C., Lecuyer, C. and Martini, M. (2000) 'Do children with autism have expectancies about the social behaviour of unfamiliar people?' *Autism 4*, 2, 133–145.

Nafstad, A. and Rødbroe, I. (1999) *Co-creating Communication.* Oslo: Forlaget-Nord Press.

Nazeer, K. (2006) *Send in the Idiots.* London: Bloomsbury Publishing.

Nind, M. and Hewett, D. (1994) *Access to Communication.* London: David Fulton.

Nind, M. and Powell, S. (2000) 'Intensive interaction and autism: Some theoretical concerns.' *Children and Society 14*, 98–109.

O'Neill, M.B. and Zeedyk, M.S. (2006) 'Spontaneous Imitation in the social interactions of young people with developmental delay and their adult carers.' *Infant and Child Development 15*, 3, 283–295.

Pelphrey, K.A., Sasson, N.J., Reznick, J.S., Paul, G., Goldman, B.D. and Piven, J. (2002) 'Visual scanning of faces in autism.' *Journal of Autism and Developmental Disorders 32*, 4, 249–261.

Potter, C. and Whittaker, C. (2001) *Enabling Communication in Children with Autism.* London: Jessica Kingsley Publishers.

Ramachandran, V., Oberman, L. and Altschuler E. (2006) 'The search for Steven.' *New Scientist*, May, 38–45.

Ramachandran, V.S. (2006) 'Broken mirrors: A theory of autism.' *Scientific American Special Issue Neuroscience 295*, 5, 39–45.

Reddy, V., Williams. E. and Vaughan, A. (2002) 'Sharing humour and laughter in autism and Down's syndrome.' *British Journal of Psychology 93*, 219–242.

Reddy, V. (2006) *Feeling Other Minds.* In preparation.

Rødbroe, I. and Souriau, J. (2000) 'Communication.' In J.M. McInnes (ed.) *A Guide to Planning and Support for Individuals who are Deaf-blind.* Toronto: University of Toronto Press.

Sigman, M. and Ungerer, J.A. (1984) 'Cognitive and Language Skills in autistic, mentally retarded and normal children.' *Developmental Psychology 20*, 293–302.

Smith, I.M. and Bryson, S.E. (1994) 'Imitation and action in autism: A critical review.' *Psychological Bulletin 116*, 259–273.

The Real Rain Man. Documentary aired on Channel Five in the UK in 2006. Bristol: Focus Productions.

Vaillant, G.R. (1993) *The Wisdom of the Ego.* Cambridge, MA: Harvard University Press.

Vege, G. 13th Jan. 2006 Presentation to Sense Scotland Seminar, Glasgow.

Vonen, A.M. and Nafstad, A. (1999) 'The concept of natural language: what does this mean for deaf-blind people?' in *The Emergence of Communication.* Suresnes, Editions du Centre National de Suresnes.

Weekes, L. (date unknown) *A Bridge of Voices.* Documentary audiotape BBC Radio 4. Produced by Tom Morton for Sandprint Programs.

Williams, D. (1993) *My Experience with Autism, Emotion and Behavior.* Documentary aired on *Eye to Eye with Connie Chung*, USA.

Williams, D. (1995) *Jam Jar.* Fresh Film, in association with Channel 4, UK.

Williams, D. (1996) *Autism: An Inside-Out Approach.* London: Jessica Kingsley Publishers.

Williams, D. (1999) *Nobody Nowhere: The Remarkable Autobiography of an Autistic Girl.* London: Jessica Kingsley Publishers.

Williams, D. (2006) *The Jumbled Jigsaw.* London: Jessica Kingsley Publishers.

Williams, R. (2005) 'The care of souls.' *Advances in Psychiatric Treatment 11*, 4–5.

Zeedyk, M.S. (2006) 'From intersubjectivity to subjectivity: The transformative roles of emotional intimacy and imitation.' *Infant and Child Development 15*, 3, 321–344.

Zeedyk, M.S. and Caldwell, P. (2006) 'Imitation promotes social engagement in adults with severe autism and learning disabilities.' Submitted to *Journal of Autism and Developmental Disabilities.*

Subject Index

Author Index